DR. & MRS. M. A. FLOTRE
3078 REVES ROAD
REGINA, SASK.
S4V 1R4

FROM ONE SHEET OF PLYWOOD

Every effort has been made to ensure that all information in this book is accurate. However, due to differing conditions, tools, and individual carpentry skills, the publisher cannot be responsible for any injuries, losses, or other damages which may result from the use of the information in this book.

Published in 1987 by Sterling Publishing Co., Inc.
Two Park Avenue, New York, NY 10016

© 1987 John Reid

A Sterling/Lark Book

Produced by Altamont Press
50 College Street, Asheville, NC 28801

ISBN 0-8069-6652-1

ISBN 0-8069-6650-5

Distributed in Canada by Oak Tree Press Company, Ltd.
c/o Canadian Manda Group, P.O. Box 920, Station U, Toronto, Ontario M8Z 5P9, Canada

Distributed in the United Kingdom by Blandford Press
Link House, West Street, Poole, Dorset BH15 1LL, England

Distributed in Australia by Capricorn Ltd.
P.O. Box 665, Lane Cove, New South Wales 2066, Australia

Printed in Hong Kong by South China Printing Company

FROM ONE SHEET OF PLYWOOD

By John Reid

A Sterling/**Lark** Book

 Sterling Publishing Co., Inc., New York

FROM ONE SHEET OF PLYWOOD
Editor: Kate Mathews
Art Director: Rob Pulleyn
Typesetting: Valerie Ward
Carpenter: Ralph Schmitt
Carpentry Assistants: Sean Trapp, Tim Mather, Robert Bauman
Photography: Dee Williams
Photographer's Assistants: John Miller, Pat Cocciadiferro
Stylists: Robin Gregory, Rob Pulleyn
Models: Robin Gregory, Kerri Bodenhamer, Sean Trapp, Adam Bodenhamer
Props: Ambiance Interiors, Stuf Antiques, WCQS Radio

Contents

Introduction

If you have been inspired to build your own architectural-style furniture after seeing the models in fashionable magazines and showrooms, you probably have wondered where to look for plans and instructions. Look no further—the projects in this book have been designed with you in mind.

The furniture you will find here is a well-rounded selection that can be dressed up or down to satisfy your unique decorating tastes. Even without previous woodworking experience, you can turn out professional-looking projects like these. The instructions for every project are detailed and complete. Each step is clearly described and is illustrated by photographs and drawings. Additionally, this introductory chapter provides the background information you need to know about the general woodworking techniques used. All required materials are clearly listed and readily available, and the required tools are common to almost every household.

To top off the enjoyment and satisfaction of building your own furniture, you will find that each and every piece is a pleasure to own. All the projects are designed to be fun and easy to make, without sacrificing updated good looks. The simple lines are sleek and modern, and they also make assembly easy. Plus, the instructions offer different finishing options, so the furniture you build will be a truly unique statement.

To understand the basic woodworking techniques you will use, read this introduction. Then you will be ready for the task of deciding just which project to make first.

PLYWOOD: THE RAW MATERIAL

Every project in this book is built from plywood—an economical, attractive, and widely available material. Plywood is manufactured from an odd number of layers or veneers of wood that are glued together with the grain directions of the layers or plies at right angles to each other. The two outside surfaces are called the face and back, the innermost layer is called the core, and the layers just beneath the face and the back are called crossbands (see Figure 1). Most plywood veneer is cut in a rotary fashion, in which a log is rotated against a blade that slices off a layer, similar to paring an apple.

The layers that comprise the crossbands and the core can vary and include bonded wood strips or chips, softwood, and other materials. Depending on which woods are used for the face and back, the result is called either hardwood or softwood plywood. Hardwood plywoods are preferred when the wood's appearance is important, as in furniture, whereas softwood plywood is extensively used in general construction.

All plywood sheets have grading stamps on their surfaces or edges that specify various features (see Figure 2). The quality or appearance of the plywood's face and back is indicated by capital letters: N (for natural finish, free of defects), A, B, C, and D, in order of descending quality of appearance. The plywood used for all projects in this book is called cabinet grade, or A-A, in which both the face and back are of high and unblemished quality. With the attractive appearance of the grain, cabinet grade plywood can be left unpainted.

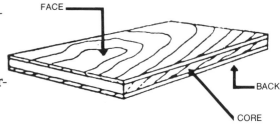

THREE-PLY VENEER CORE CONSTRUCTION

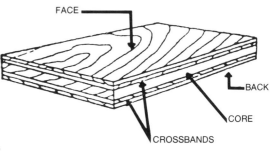

FIVE-PLY VENEER CORE CONSTRUCTION

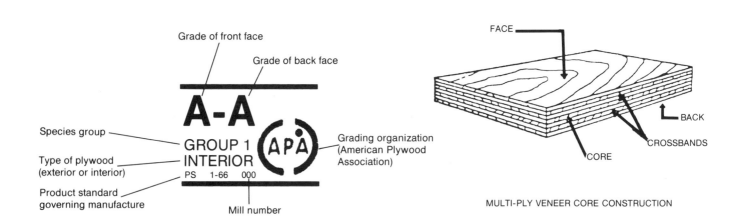

MULTI-PLY VENEER CORE CONSTRUCTION

Figure 2. Plywood Grading Stamp

Grade of front face
Grade of back face
Species group
Type of plywood (exterior or interior)
Product standard governing manufacture

A-A
GROUP 1
INTERIOR
PS 1-66 000

Grading organization (American Plywood Association)
Mill number

Figure 1. Plywood Construction

Plywood is made from an odd number of wood layers that are glued together so the grain directions of the layers are at right angles to each other. Courtesy Hardwood Plywood Manufacturers Association.

The relative strength of the woods used in manufacturing the plywood is indicated by the group number. Group 1 indicates the strongest varieties of wood, and Group 5 indicates the weakest. (Figure 3 lists varieties of wood species in each group.) The plywood used for the projects in this book is birch veneer, from Group 1.

Plywood is also specified as Exterior or Interior. This rating indicates the durability of the glue bonds between the layers of veneer. The adhesives used in Exterior grades are waterproof, while those used in Interior grades are water resistant, but not waterproof. Items made from Interior grade plywood should not be used outdoors. The plywood used for the projects in this book is Interior.

Figure 3. Groups of Woods Commonly Used to Make Plywood

Group 1	Group 2	Group 3	Group 4	Group 5
Ash, white	Ash, black	Alder, red	Aspen	Fir, balsam
Apitong	Avodire	Basswood, American	Cedar, Eastern red	Poplar
Beech, American	Birch, paper	Butternut	Cedar, Western red	
Birch, yellow, sweet	Cherry, black	Cativo	Fuma	
Bubinga	Cypress	Chestnut, American	Willow, black	
Hickory	Elm, rock	Cottonwood, black		
Kapur	Fir, Douglas	Cottonwood, Eastern		
Keruing	Fir, white	Elm, American (grey, red or white)		
Oak (Oregon, red or white)	Gum, sweet	Gum, black		
Paldao	Hemlock, Western	Hackberry		
Pecan	Magnolia, Cucumber Sweetbay	Hemlock, Eastern		
Rosewood	Maple, sugar (hard)	Lauan		
Sapele	Mahogany, African	Maple, red (soft)		
	Mahogany, Honduras	Maple, silver (soft)		
	Maple, black (hard)	Meranti, red		
	Pine, Western white	Pine, ponderosa		
	Poplar, yellow	Pine, sugar		
	Spruce, red, Sitka	Pine, Eastern white		
	Sycamore	Prima-vera		
	Tanoak	Redwood		
	Teak	Sassafras		
	Walnut, American	Spruce, black, Engelmann, white		
		Tupelo, water		

The relative strengths of woods used in plywood are graded in descending order, from Group 1 to Group 5. Identification of wood refers to the species used in the plywood's face. Courtesy Hardwood Plywood Manufacturers Association.

MEASURING

The first step of every project in this book is to measure and mark all pieces on the plywood. The importance of correct measuring cannot be overemphasized. Carefully measured pieces fit together correctly the first time, so that second cuts are unnecessary and materials are not wasted. The carpenter's saying, "Measure twice and cut once," is a good one to remember and practice!

Before measuring, check the dimensions of the materials you are starting out with. Just as the actual dimensions of a 2x4 piece of lumber are not the same as its nominal dimensions, a sheet of 3/4" plywood may actually measure 11/16". This variation will affect assembly details like the size of dado grooves in which plywood shelves must fit and the size of router bits that are used to make those dado grooves.

When measuring, the saw kerf, or width of the groove made by a cutting tool, must be taken into account. It is safe to assume a minimum loss of 1/16" for each saw kerf. Therefore, in the case of cutting a 4' width into four equal pieces, the actual dimensions of each piece may be slightly less than 12". To compensate for this, divide the entire 4' width into four equal sections rather than measuring 12" widths, starting from one edge. This eliminates the possibility of ending up with three 12" pieces and one 11¾" piece.

There are a variety of tools to facilitate measuring. This book calls for a combination square, T-bevel, and compass or string and pencil. The combination square is a versatile tool, used for measuring, marking straight lines, and defining 45° and 90° angles. It also has one or two levels built right into it. The adjustable T-bevel is used to measure and mark angles of any degree. A compass or string and pencil is used to mark curves evenly and quickly, useful for round chair seats.

In this book, dimensions are indicated on the various assembly diagrams for each project. However, dimensions can be adjusted to adapt to your needs or preferences. For example, cabinets can be deeper or taller, tables can be smaller, shelves can be fewer, or chair backs can be higher. When altering any dimensions, check carefully to determine which components require adjustment.

NOTE:
In ALL Cutting Diagrams, ½" equals 1'.
In ALL Assembly Diagrams, ¼" equals 4".

METRIC EQUIVALENCY
CM=CENTIMETERS
INCHES TO CENTIMETERS

INCHES	CM
⅛	0.3
¼	0.6
⅜	1.0
½	1.3
⅝	1.6
¾	1.9
⅞	2.2
1	2.5
1¼	3.2
1½	3.8
1¾	4.4
2	5.1
2½	6.4
3	7.6
3½	8.9
4	10.2
4½	11.4
5	12.7
6	15.2
7	17.8
8	20.3
9	22.9
10	25.4
11	27.9
12	30.5
13	33.0
14	35.6
15	38.1
16	40.6
17	43.2
18	45.7
19	48.3
20	50.8
21	53.3
22	55.9
23	58.4
24	61.0
25	63.5
26	66.0
27	68.6
28	71.1
29	73.7
30	76.2
31	78.7
32	81.3
33	83.8
34	86.4
35	88.9
36	91.4
37	94.0
38	96.5
39	99.1
40	101.6
41	104.1
42	106.7
43	109.2
44	111.8
45	114.3
46	116.8
47	119.4
48	121.9
49	124.5
50	127.0

CUTTING

When all pieces have been carefully measured and marked on the plywood, cutting is a simple task. Rough cuts, indicated by circled numbers in the cutting diagrams in this book, are made first, to separate the plywood sheet into easily manageable pieces.

Because many parts of each project will be unpainted, it is recommended that you take advantage of the wood's attractive grain whenever possible, especially on doors and table-tops. Simply adjust the arrangement of pieces on the plywood, before cutting. Note that the cutting diagrams in this book identify how many of each piece must be cut.

The cutting tools commonly available in most households—an electric circular saw and saber saw—are needed to make the projects in this book. The circular saw is used for all straight cuts and the saber saw makes the more intricate cuts and curved shapes. Use of a hollow ground saw blade is advised for work with plywood, since it makes the smoothest cut and leaves very few saw marks. Naturally, you will want to keep an extra sharp blade or two on hand, so that you never have to cut with a dull blade.

Every project in this book can be made with hand-held tools. However, the use of a table saw and radial arm saw will greatly facilitate cutting small or repetitive pieces and is recommended for certain projects. Extreme caution and standard safety measures should be exercised at all times when working with any power tools. Remove jewelry, scarves, or anything that may get caught or in the way. Protect eyes from flying chips and sawdust by wearing goggles. Follow all safety instructions that come with every tool you use.

The ability to make absolutely straight cuts is crucial to proper fit, correct size, and the good looks of the product. To assure straight cuts, a cutting guide is used in most projects. The cutting guide is clamped in place along the line to be cut and the sole plate or base plate of the saw is run right along the guide to make a straight and clean cut. The projects in this book call for cutting guides in 4', 6', and 8' lengths.

To make a cutting guide, glue a narrow piece of ¾" plywood on top of a wider piece of ¼" plywood. Rest the sole plate or base plate of the circular saw along the inside edge of the ¾" piece and cut off the excess width of the ¼" piece. Clamp the cut edge along any line, with the saw's sole plate resting against the inside edge, and you will make straight and true cuts.

While every effort has been made to use up all the plywood in every project, scraps and leftover pieces will inevitably occur. Don't discard them—many small pieces can be cut from scraps and several projects in this book were especially designed to use up scraps.

ASSEMBLY

The projects in this book employ a limited number of assembly techniques, for the sake of simplicity and consistency. Pieces may be joined by glue and nails, glue and dowels, or screws. Dado grooves are made with a router and a straight bit that is ¾" or the size that fits the plywood width; pieces fit or slide into the dado grooves for a tight fit. Doors are attached with hinges and folding parts use hinges for ease of operation.

The use of glue and clamps is an important preliminary step that readies pieces for permanent joinery. Select a water resistant white or yellow wood glue, apply sparingly, and always allow sufficient drying time before going on to the next assembly step.

The clamps called for in this book are C-clamps and bar clamps. C-clamps are available in a variety of sizes (4" and/or 6" clamps will be usedful for these projects). Always insert wood scraps between the clamp jaws and the wood you're working with, to protect the wood's finish. Bar clamps are adjustable across wider surfaces and are therefore invaluable for clamping larger pieces.

Finishing nails (without heads) are specified in this book, since they are always set below the surface and the resulting holes filled with wood filler. The nail sizes most commonly used in this book are 3d (1¼"), 4d (1½"), and 6d (2"). The letter "d" is the British abbreviation for "pence," and because nails were very inexpensive, the term "penny" became the standard measurement for nail sizes. While "penny" remains the standard of measurement today, it signifies length rather than price.

The screws called for in this book are flathead wood screws in lengths of 1¼"-2". Screws must be selected for length and also for gauge or shank diameter. Common screws range in gauges of 2-16; this book calls for #6 or #8. When using screws to assemble pieces, it is wise to drill a pilot or starter hole of a diameter slightly less than the screw itself, to facilitate insertion of the screw and avoid splitting the wood.

Doweled assembly gives a very sturdy joint, and one that is attractive enough to be used as a design feature. Always glue and clamp the pieces together first, and when the glue is completely dry, drill holes at periodic points along the glued joint. The intervals between drill holes can be equidistant or irregular, as long as they are close enough to provide a strong joint. The instructions in this book call for drill holes to be approximately 2" apart and 2½" deep, to accommodate the lengths of dowel that are glued and tapped into them.

Piano hinges, or continuous hinges, are specified in this book. When substantial weight must be supported, piano hinges are advised. However, when a small or lightweight door is to be attached, cabinet or ornamental hinges may be substituted. Most hinges come with screws that fit them precisely, and piano hinges have pre-drilled holes 2" apart. For ease of handling and for symmetrical appearance, cut piano hinges exactly between the pre-drilled holes, using a hack saw.

NAIL SIZES

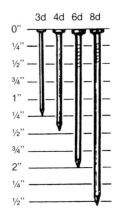

FLATHEAD WOOD SCREWS

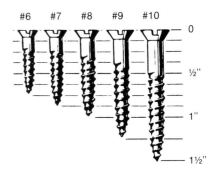

FINISHING

Once the project is built, it must be properly finished to highlight its beauty and preserve the condition of the wood. This is also the step that turns a basic piece of furniture into something special, puts your individual touch on it, adds pizzazz, or blends it in with the surrounding decor.

It is important to first check all glued, nailed, and doweled joints. Nails should be set slightly below the surface and the resulting holes filled with wood filler; dowel ends should be sanded until smooth and flush with the surface. Additionally, any gaps or roughness in the edges of the plywood should be filled with wood filler and sanded smooth.

When all surfaces, edges, and joints are smooth, clear or opaque finishes can be applied. This book calls for polyurethane varnish and oil base enamel paint. Polyurethane varnish is a tough plastic varnish that gives a durable and moisture-resistant surface. Select from matte, semigloss, or high gloss finishes, according to preference and appropriateness to the particular project, such as furniture or gymnasium floors.

In this book, turpentine or paint thinner is used to slightly thin the polyurethane for ease of application and to avoid thick build-up of coats. Apply polyurethane with a brush and allow to dry thoroughly, from overnight up to 24 hours. Lightly sand with fine grit sandpaper between each coat, to create a slightly roughened surface that improves adhesion of the next applied coat. Lightly buff the last coat with fine steel wool, for a final touch of smoothness.

Oil base enamel paint gives the most durable finish and is available in brilliant colors. The type of enamel paint used in the book is sign and bulletin paint. As with polyurethane varnish, paint adheres better if lightly sanded between coats. Choices of paint color and placement are completely open to your preferences, and methods of paint application can be varied, from speckling and stenciling, to texturizing and antiquing. Here's your chance to use your imagination to create unique looks.

INSTRUCTION EXAMPLE

In the following Floor Lamp project, which appears on page 117, you will see examples of the different parts of every project in this book. The combination of written instructions and scale drawings makes it easier to visualize the product and to understand all assembly steps.

Instructions are separated into Cutting, Assembly, and Finishing steps for convenient reference. Special notes are used where needed to indicate when extra care is required, a carpentry tip will be helpful, or an alternative method can be used.

Materials and tools required for all projects are clearly listed. If a project can be assembled from leftover plywood scraps, it is indicated as such along with the amount needed if full plywood sheets are used. All materials are available at most general hardware stores and all tools are commonly available in most households.

Cutting Diagrams indicate how many of each piece will be needed and how to arrange the cutting layout to avoid waste. When altering dimensions or taking advantage of the wood's attractive grain, the cutting layout can be adjusted. Refer to the Cutting Diagrams and Assembly Diagrams to verify dimensions and measure carefully before cutting. The scale used in all Cutting Diagrams is: ½" = 1'.

Assembly Diagrams show front and side views of the project, as well as exploded views of specific portions of the project. Instructions make references to specific diagrams, to clarify assembly steps and guarantee understanding. The scale used in all Assembly Diagrams is: ¼" = 4".

Finishing steps describe how the project shown was handled. Alternative suggestions for finishing are provided, to achieve different results. For a personalized look, experiment with the many different finishing options.

Floor Lamp Adds a Soft Touch

This statuesque floor lamp glows with a soft beauty that adds warmth to any corner. The layers of colored plastic sandwiched between the plywood create a halo-like effect when illuminated by the single bulb. The clean architectural lines of the lamp are just right for today's contemporary decorating trends. To top off such elegant looks, this lamp is great for using up plywood scraps left over from other projects in this book.

INSTRUCTIONS:

Cutting

NOTE: Use of a table saw or radial arm saw will make cutting small pieces much easier.

Measure and mark all pieces on plywood and tinted thermoplastic. Cut Sides with cutting guide clamped in place to assure straight cuts.

Using router and ¾" bit, cut dado grooves ⅛" deep where shown in Assembly Diagram. Lay Sides upright on their edges and measure width from dado groove to dado groove. Cut Shelves to fit these dimensions. **NOTE:** Other pieces will be cut after Sides and Shelves are assembled.

Locate and mark the center of each shelf. Drill hole for a snug fit around lamp cord at each center. **NOTE:** When drilling holes, make certain the back side of the plywood is in contact with a flat piece of scrap board. Move the scrap board between drillings for a fresh flat surface. This prevents splintering of the plywood face.

Assembly

Assemble Shelves to Sides with glue and nails. Set nails 1/16" below surface and fill with wood filler. When dry, sand until smooth and flush with surface.

Measure exact dimensions for Base Front and Base Back; cut these pieces with cutting guide clamped in place. Cut hole in Base Back for on-off switch or dimmer switch. Install Base Front and Base Back between Sides with glue and nails. Set nails and fill holes as above.

To assemble Shade, cut tinted thermoplastic squares and plywood squares. Mark and drill ½" holes where shown in Cutting Diagram. Connect outside circumference of the drilled holes, to make a square; using saber saw, cut out square shape. With router and ½" bit, trim the inside of the square shape (this assures that light will pass through the thermoplastic smoothly). **NOTE:** Thermoplastic and plywood layers for Shade may also be cut and assembled

Materials

2/3 sheet (or ½ sheet plus scraps) ¾" cabinet grade birch veneer plywood
Tinted Acrilite GP or Plexiglas thermoplastic
Porcelain lamp socket
On-off switch or dimmer switch
8'-10' lamp cord
Plug
Silvered bowl light bulb
3d finishing nails
1¼" x #6 flathead wood screws
Waterproof wood glue
Contact cement, to assemble layers of shade
Acetone, to glue tinted thermoplastic
Wood filler
Sandpaper, fine/80 grit
Polyurethane varnish or sealer
Turpentine or paint thinner
Oil base enamel, with eggshell finish, in color of choice

Tools

Electric circular saw with hollow ground plywood blade
Electric variable speed drill with ½″ and size to fit lamp cord auger-type bits
Saber saw
Router with ½″ straight bit and ¾″ straight bit or size to fit plywood thickness
Combination square, for measuring and marking
Nail set
Cutting guides, 4′ and 8′

from narrow strips; glue thermoplastic strips with acetone and plywood strips with wood glue to form squares.

Using contact cement, glue Shade layers together. Screw Shade to top of lamp. Install porcelain socket, lamp cord, switch, plug, and silvered bowl light bulb.

Finishing

Make sure all nails are set 1/16″ below surface. Fill all nail holes, cracks, and joints. Sand until completely smooth. Apply one coat of polyurethane varnish or sealer to all plywood parts; when dry, sand and check all fillings for smoothness. Using oil base enamel in color of choice, paint with two coats, sanding lightly between coats.

If the grain of the plywood is particularly attractive, finish the lamp clear, using 1 part turpentine or paint thinner to 3 parts polyurethane varnish in three coats, lightly sanding between coats and buffing with fine steel wool after the final coat.

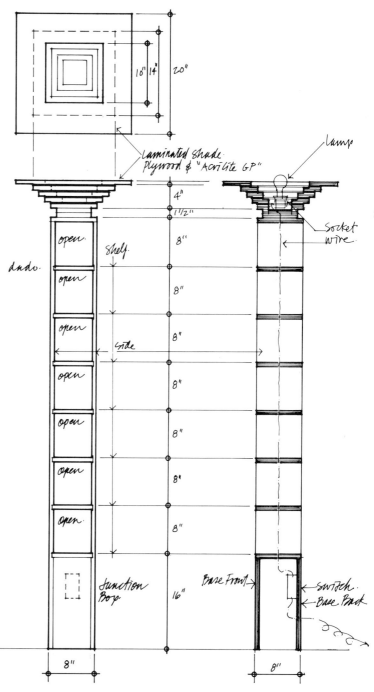

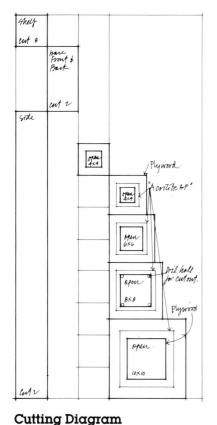

Cutting Diagram

Assembly Diagram

Make the Most
out of Hallway Space

Make the Most out of Hallway Space

If you have plenty of hallway space, but not much in the way of storage space, here's a perfect piece. This bench is especially designed for a hallway and offers a comfortable stop to tie shoes, look over the mail, or enjoy a favorite book. Underneath its hinged seats is plenty of storage space, and the handy shelf units that double as arms make even more room for books, telephone, or knick-knacks. Its modular design makes it easy to disassemble and move it to a new spot or a new home.

INSTRUCTIONS:

Cutting

Measure and mark all pieces on plywood. Make rough cuts as indicated by circled numbers in Cutting Diagrams to separate plywood into manageable pieces, with cutting guide clamped in place to assure straight cuts.

Mark and cut all pieces of the Arm units to width, with cutting guide clamped in place. Using router, make dado grooves where shown in Cutting Diagram 2. Cut dowels into 2½" lengths. Using hack saw, cut piano hinge following dimensions in Assembly Diagram 1.

Assembly

Prop Arm Front and Arm Back upright on work surface; position Arm Top, Shelf, and Bottom between Front and Back, in the dado grooves. Glue and clamp in place; drill ¼" holes approximately 2½" deep and 3" apart. Apply glue to holes and to dowel lengths; tap dowels into holes. When glue is dry, sand dowel ends until smooth and flush with surface. Cut Arm Base; glue and clamp to Arm unit as shown in Assembly Diagram 2. Glue and dowel as above.

Cut all pieces for Seat units, with cutting guide clamped in place. Prop Seat Sides upright on working surface. Position Seat Bottom, Seat Front, and Seat Back between Sides. Glue and clamp in place; when glue is dry, glue and dowel as above.

Screw Seat ledges to Seat Sides, as shown in Assembly Diagram 2. Glue and dowel Fixed Seat piece to Sides and Back. Using awl or ice pick to start screw holes, attach hinge to rear edge of Hinged Seat; attach Hinged Seat to Fixed Seat piece.

From the inside, screw the two Seat units together side-to-side. Cut Front Base and Back Base pieces to full arm-to-arm length; screw Front Base and Back Base to each Arm Unit (see Assembly Diagram 2). Place Seat units on Base between Arm units; from inside, screw Seat units to Base.

Finishing

NOTE: For ease of finishing, remove Seat units and Base from Arm units. Finish each component separately and then reassemble.

Using a mixture of 1 part turpentine or paint thinner to 3 parts polyurethane varnish, finish all components with 3 coats, sanding lightly between coats and buffing with fine steel wool after the final coat.

Alternative design options include altering the shapes of the Back pieces, painting all or various parts with 3 coats of oil base enamel in color of your choice, padding the arms, or adding seat cushions.

Materials

1-2/3 4'x8' sheet, or 1 - 4'x8' sheet plus scraps, ¾" cabinet grade birch veneer plywood
1 - 4' length piano hinge
¼" dowels
1½" x #8 flathead wood screws
Waterproof wood glue
Polyurethane varnish
Turpentine or paint thinner
Sandpaper, fine/80 grit
Fine steel wool

Tools

Electric circular saw with hollow ground plywood blade
Electric variable speed drill with ¼" auger-type bit
Router with ¾" straight bit, or size to fit plywood width
Hack saw, for cutting piano hinge
Bar clamps
Awl or ice pick
Screwdriver appropriate for screws that come with piano hinges
Cutting guides, 4' and 8'

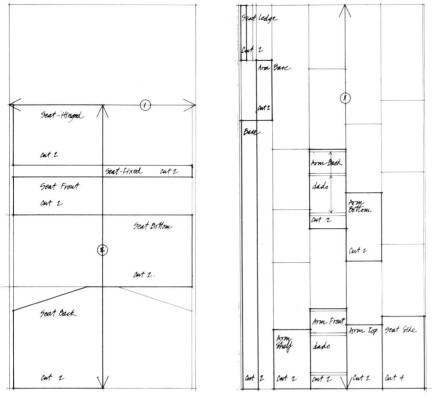

Cutting Diagram 1

Cutting Diagram 2

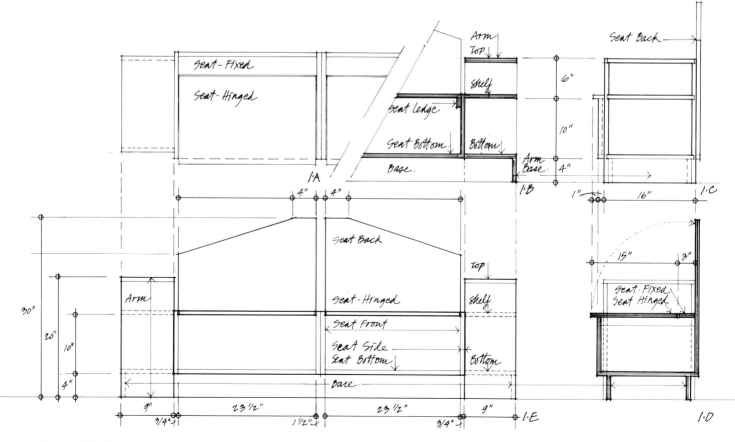

Assembly Diagram 1

(Instructions continued on page 22)

A Handy Perch for Breakfast Bar or Drafting Table

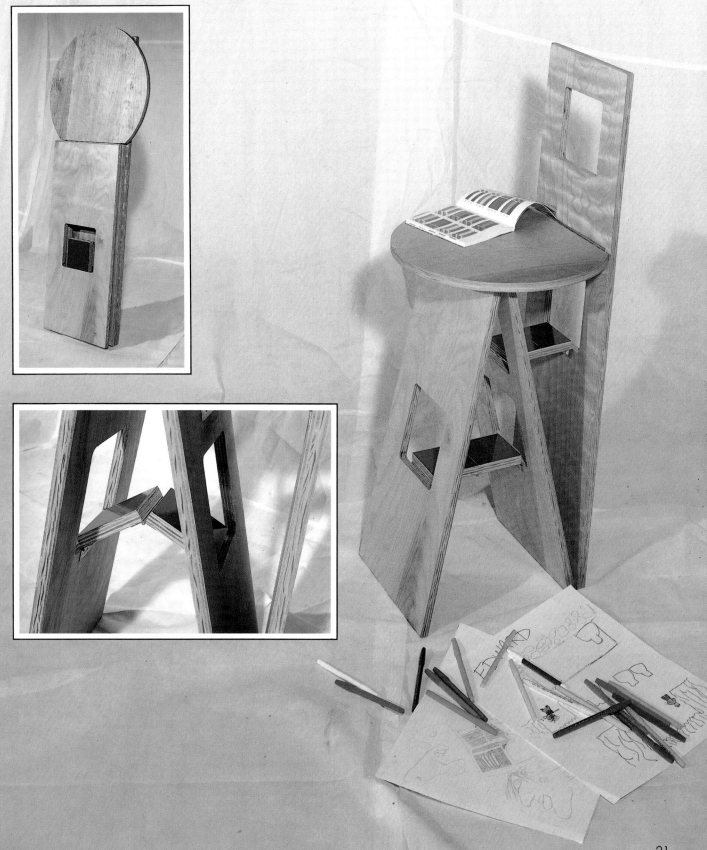

(Hall Bench, continued from page 19)

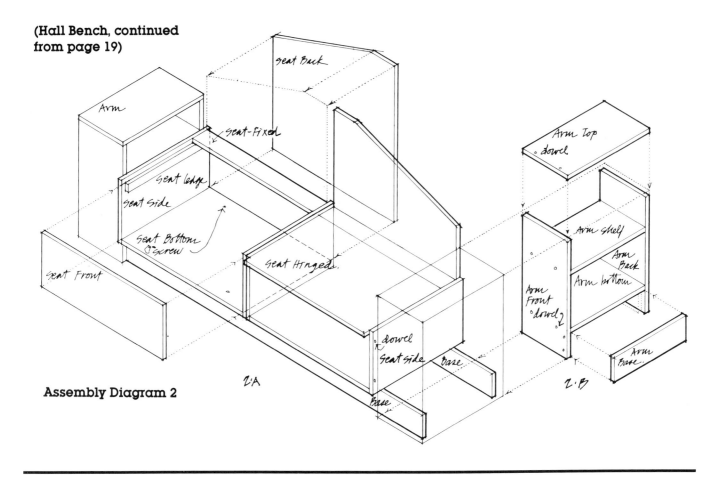

Assembly Diagram 2

A Handy Perch for Breakfast Bar or Drafting Table

If you have a breakfast bar or a drafting table (maybe you've already made the one in this book), you know how important it is to have the right chair or stool. Not only is this spiffy stool the right height—important for comfort and being able to work without fatigue—it folds up in an instant for storing or toting. And, it even has a built-in handle and footrest! If you want a matching set, you're in luck—you can cut a pair from one plywood sheet.

INSTRUCTIONS:

Cutting

NOTE: One sheet of plywood yields all pieces for two stools, plus scraps. An alternate cutting option is to cut all legs and backs for four stools from one plywood sheet, and cut seats from other wood or a second plywood sheet.

Measure and mark all pieces on plywood sheet. Make rough cut 1 (indicated by circled number) to separate plywood into manageable pieces, with cutting guide clamped in place to assure straight cuts. Mark and cut Legs and Backs, with cutting guide clamped in place.

Mark and drill holes for cutouts in Backs and Legs, following Assembly Diagram 1-B. **NOTE:** When drilling holes, make certain the back side of the plywood is in contact with a flat piece of scrap board. Move the scrap board between drillings for a fresh flat surface. This prevents splintering of the plywood face. Connect outer circumferences of the drilled holes, to make squares. Using saber saw, cut out squares. Using compass or string and pencil, mark curved Seat (see Assembly Diagram 1-A); cut out with saber saw.

Using hack saw, cut hinges to fit dimensions of Seat and Cross Braces. **NOTE:** Piano hinges come with pre-drilled holes 2 inches apart; cut hinges exactly between holes for ease of handling.

Materials

1 - 4'x8' sheet ¾" cabinet grade birch veneer plywood
1 - 6' length piano hinge for each stool
1 quart polyurethane varnish
Turpentine or paint thinner
Sandpaper, fine/80 grit
Fine steel wool

Tools

Electric circular saw with hollow
   ground plywood blade
Electric variable speed drill with ½"
   auger-type bit
Saber saw, for cutting curved seat and
   leg cutouts
Hack saw, for cutting hinges
Compass or string and pencil, for
   marking curved seat
Awl or ice pick
Screwdriver appropriate for screws
   that come with piano hinges
Cutting guide, 4'

Assembly

Using awl or ice pick to start screw holes, hinge Back Leg to Back at floor level (see Assembly Diagram 1-D), and then hinge Front Leg to Back Leg at seat level. Hinge pairs of Front Cross Brace pieces together; attach hinges to outside edges of hinged Cross Braces. Attach each edge of hinged Front Cross Brace to its matching leg (remove screws from center hinge to facilitate access). Attach Back Cross Braces between Back Leg and Back in the same way (see Assembly Diagram 1-C). Attach hinge to back edge of Seat, and then to Back.

Finishing

Using a mixture of 1 part turpentine or paint thinner to 3 parts polyurethane varnish, finish stool with three coats. Allow each coat to dry thoroughly. Lightly sand between coats, and buff lightly with steel wool after final coat.

For an alternative to a clear finish, lightly pad and upholster seat (seat won't fold flat when upholstered), or substitute readymade 1950s-type kitchen seats for a very fresh look.

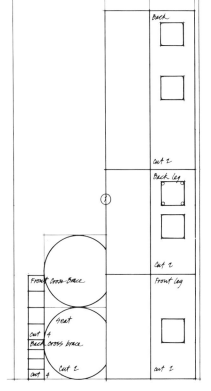

Cutting Diagram

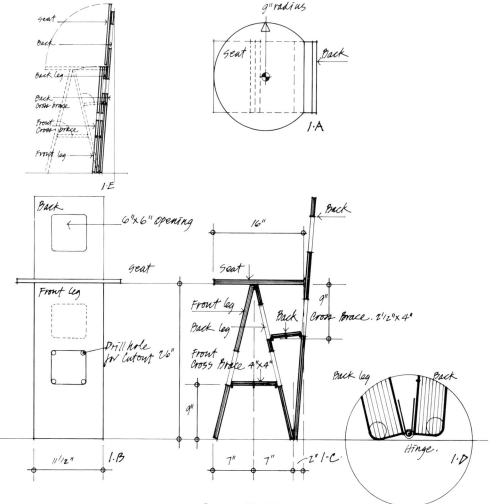

Assembly Diagram

23

Stacking Chairs Accented with Color

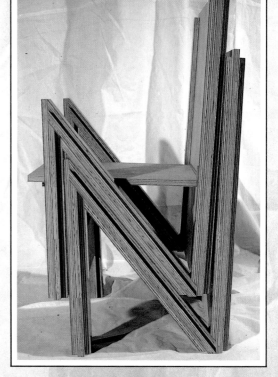

Stacking Chairs Accented with Color

If you're looking for chairs that are easy to store, yet sturdier than folding chairs, you'll want to build these attractive stacking chairs. They provide a solid seat, and the painted trim adds an exclamation point of color that makes them stand out in a crowd. When they're not needed, just stack them up in an out-of-the-way place.

INSTRUCTIONS:

Cutting

NOTE: Many pieces can be cut from scraps. A table saw or radial arm saw will make cutting legs and small pieces much easier.

Measure, mark, and draw chair to full scale on working surface. Measure and mark all pieces on plywood. Make rough cuts 1 and 2 (indicated by circled numbers) to separate plywood into manageable pieces, with cutting guide clamped in place to assure straight cuts.

Calculate how many lineal feet of various sizes of Leg, Trim, and diagonal Leg Brace will be needed. Rough cut these lengths.

Using hack saw, cut piano hinge to fit seat dimension. **NOTE:** Piano hinges come with pre-drilled holes 2 inches apart; cut hinges exactly between holes for ease of handling.

Assembly

Assemble Front Leg, Seat Ledge, and Leg Brace in layers, in the sequence shown in Assembly Diagram 2-A, making finish cuts to length and angle as you go. Before applying top layer of trim, drive a #8 wood screw through the Front Leg and Leg Brace as shown in Assembly Diagram 1-D. Nail trim in place; set nails 1/16" below surface. Fill holes with wood filler; when dry, sand until smooth and flush with surface.

Compare Front Leg/Leg Brace assembly to full scale drawing to determine if adjustments to Back Leg are needed. Attach Back Leg to Leg Brace in layers, as above. Drive a #8 wood screw through the Back Leg and Leg Brace as shown in Assembly Diagram 1-C. Mark location of Seat; attach Seat to Back with hinge, using awl or ice pick to start screw holes. Using #6 screws, attach Lip to underside of seat as shown in Assembly Diagram 1-A (Lip keeps chair rigid).

Finishing

Using a mixture of 1 part turpentine or paint thinner to 3 parts polyurethane varnish, finish unpainted parts of Chair with three coats. Allow each coat to dry thoroughly. Lightly sand between coats, and buff lightly with steel wool after final coat. Paint Trim with three coats of oil base enamel in color(s) of your choice, sanding lightly between coats.

Materials

1 - 4'x8' sheet ¾" cabinet grade birch veneer plywood
1 - 4' length piano hinge
3d finishing nails
1¼" x #6 flathead wood screws
#8 flathead wood screws, at least 2" long
Wood filler
Polyurethane varnish
Turpentine or paint thinner
Oil base enamel in color of choice
Sandpaper, fine/80 grit
Fine steel wool

Tools

Electric circular saw with hollow ground plywood blade
Hack saw, for cutting piano hinge
Nail set
Awl or ice pick
Screwdriver appropriate for screws that come with piano hinges
Cutting guide, 4'

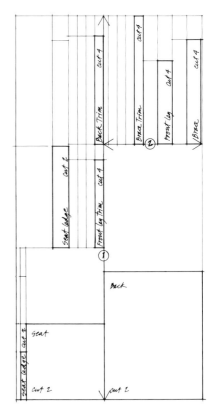

Cutting Diagram

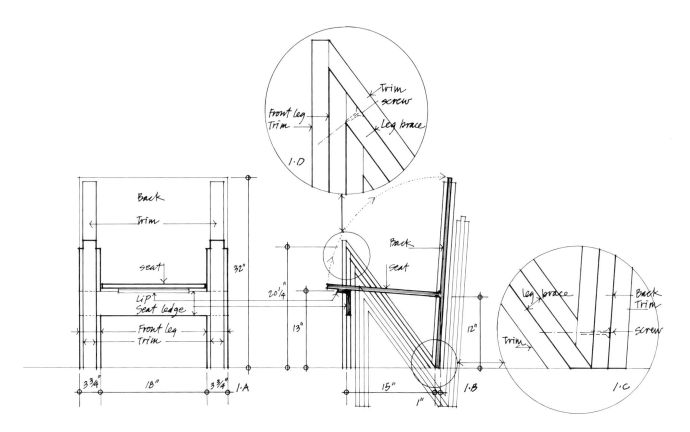

Assembly Diagram 1

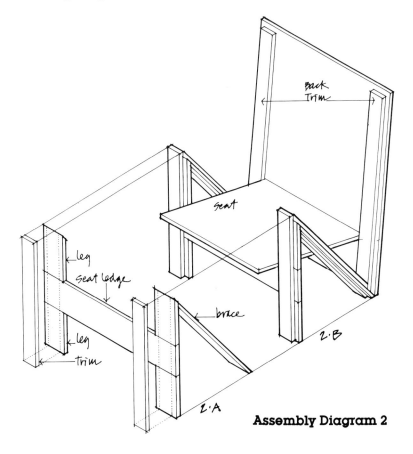

Assembly Diagram 2

A Couch That Flexes
With Your Lifestyle

A Couch That Flexes With Your Lifestyle

This easy-to-build four-piece unit is as flexible as you need it to be. Arrange it as a luxurious futon couch piled high with pillows—it has two matching occasional tables and handy magazine storage space underneath. When guests arrive for a visit, transform the couch into a generous and healthful bed. This versatile design is well-suited to any room size and every decorating scheme.

INSTRUCTIONS:

Cutting

NOTE: The standard height for a seat of this depth is 15-16 inches from the floor to the top of the cushion. If your futon, when folded and "flattened," is less than seven inches thick, adjust the height measurements of the Seat Base Backs, Seat Sides, Seat Backs, and Table Sides to achieve the overall seat height. It is advisable to have your futon and pillows or cushions on hand prior to marking and cutting plywood.

When dimensions are determined, measure and mark all pieces on plywood sheets. Make four rough cuts (indicated by circled numbers) to separate plywood into manageable pieces, with cutting guide clamped in place to assure straight cuts. Cut all pieces, with cutting guide clamped in place.

Assembly

Glue and clamp Table Bottoms to Table Sides; glue and clamp Seat Bottoms to Seat Sides and Seat Base Backs. When glue is dry, cut dowels into 1½" lengths. Turn assemblies over and drill holes 2" deep, approximately 6" apart, along glued and clamped edges. Apply glue to dowels and into holes, tap dowels into holes until flush with surface, to permanently join bottoms to sides and backs. Allow glue to dry. Glue and nail 2½"x2½" pedestals to Seat Bottoms and Table Bottoms.

Turn assemblies over. Glue and dowel Seat Tops and Table Tops in place; allow glue to dry. Glue and nail Back Ledges to Seat Base Backs, flush with bottom edge (this ledge allows for easier installation and removal of the Seat Backs).

Cut out curved edge of Seat Back with saber saw. **Do not** trim bottom edge of Seat Backs yet. Fold and flatten your futon and place it, along with the stacked pillows, on the Seat units. Holding each Seat Back in place, mark where to trim so that when Seat Back is resting on the Back Ledge, it clears the top pillow (see photos). Trim Seat Backs along bottom edge where marked; screw into Seat Base Backs.

Materials

4 - 4'x8' sheets ¾" cabinet grade birch veneer plywood
3d finishing nails
1½" x #10 flathead wood screws,
5/16" wood dowels
Waterproof wood glue
Polyurethane varnish
Turpentine or paint thinner
Paste wax
Sandpaper, fine/80 grit
Fine steel wool

Tools

Electric circular saw with hollow ground plywood blade
Saber saw
Electric variable speed drill with 5/16" auger-type bit
8" C-clamps, or bar clamps
Combination square
Cutting guide, 5'

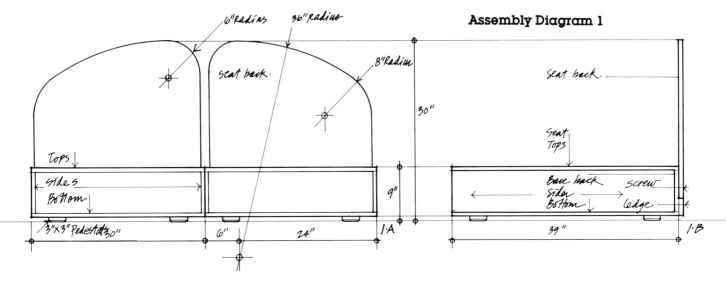

Assembly Diagram 1

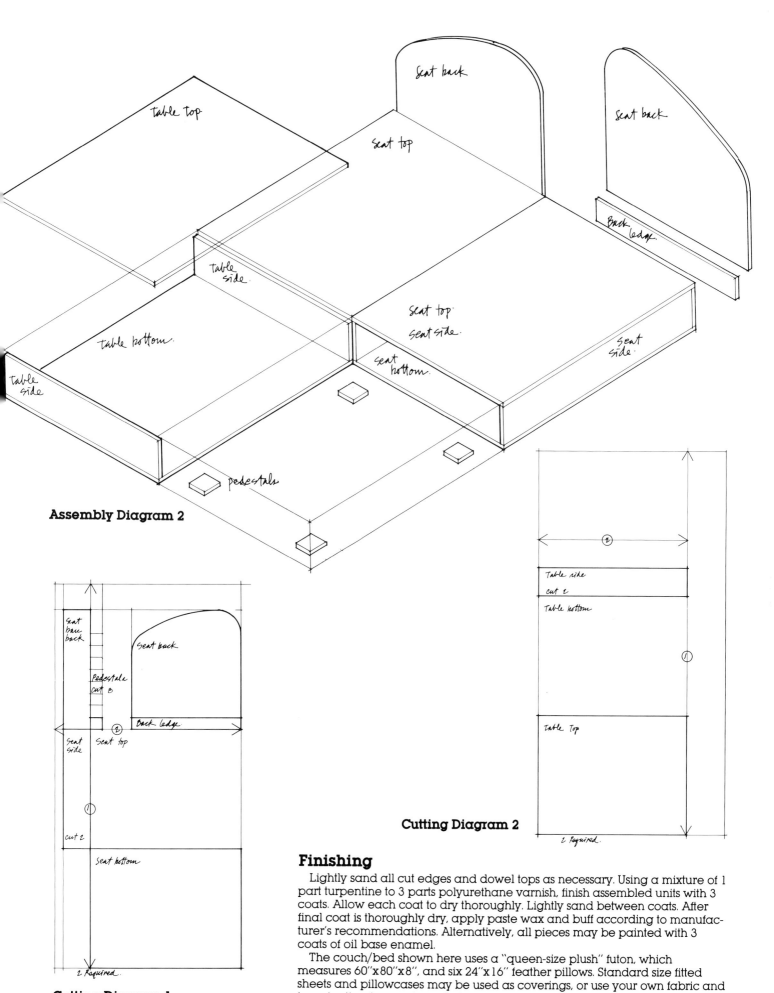

Assembly Diagram 2

Cutting Diagram 1

Cutting Diagram 2

Finishing

Lightly sand all cut edges and dowel tops as necessary. Using a mixture of 1 part turpentine to 3 parts polyurethane varnish, finish assembled units with 3 coats. Allow each coat to dry thoroughly. Lightly sand between coats. After final coat is thoroughly dry, apply paste wax and buff according to manufacturer's recommendations. Alternatively, all pieces may be painted with 3 coats of oil base enamel.

The couch/bed shown here uses a "queen-size plush" futon, which measures 60"x80"x8", and six 24"x16" feather pillows. Standard size fitted sheets and pillowcases may be used as coverings, or use your own fabric and imagination for a unique design.

Unfolding Good Taste

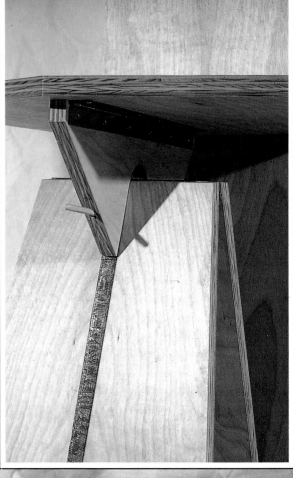

Unfolding Good Taste

Most folding chairs are uninteresting in their design, right? Not these freshly asymmetrical chairs—they look so good, you may never stow them away in a closet. They're easy to build, sleek, and they fold flat in an instant. While economical in design—four can be cut from one sheet of plywood—they are rich in today's architectural styling. Whether clear finished, painted, or upholstered, they will come in handy at all your parties, card games, and dinners—no matter how large the guest list!

INSTRUCTIONS, Folding Chair 1:
Cutting

NOTE: Four chairs may be cut from one piece of plywood. However, if you rearrange the cutting layout to take advantage of the wood's attractive grain, you can cut Chair Backs and Chair Seats from one sheet and build Front Legs and Hinged Arms from scrap plywood, or you can buy two sheets of plywood.

Measure and mark all pieces on plywood sheet. Make rough cuts 1, 2, and 3 (indicated by circled numbers) to separate plywood into manageable pieces, with cutting guide clamped in place to assure straight cuts.

Mark and cut Backs, with cutting guide clamped in place. Mark and cut Front Legs, with cutting guide clamped in place. Mark and cut Hinged Arms and Seats, with cutting guide clamped in place.

Mark curved edges of Seats, using compass or string and pencil for smooth curve. Cut curved edges, using saber saw. Clamp a straight board to each seat bottom, to act as guide for routing ¼"-deep slot that fits over Front Leg and fixes Seat in open position.

Cut hinges to fit dimensions of Seat and Hinged Arm. **NOTE:** Piano hinges come with pre-drilled holes 2 inches apart; cut hinges exactly between two pre-drilled holes for ease of handling.

Assembly

Mark hinge locations on all pieces, following Assembly Diagrams 1-A and 1-B. Using awl or ice pick to start screw holes, attach hinges to Backs, then to back edges of Seats.

Using awl or ice pick to start screw holes, attach hinges to Back and Hinged Arm. Attach hinges to Hinged Arm and Front Leg. **OPTIONAL:** Attach sliding bolt or window latch to underside of each Seat, to lock it to Front Leg in open position.

Finishing

Using a mixture of 1 part turpentine or paint thinner to 3 parts polyurethane varnish, finish chairs with three coats. Allow each coat to dry thoroughly. Lightly sand between coats, and buff lightly with steel wool after final coat.

For design variations, clear finish all flat surfaces of the chairs and paint the edges in a bright accent color. Paint all chair parts in one color, or use different colors on the various parts to add interest to the chair in its folded and unfolded positions. Lightly pad and upholster seats and backs (chairs will not fold flat when upholstered). Use seat and back shapes from other chairs in this book, or vary shapes according to your imagination.

INSTRUCTIONS, Folding Chair 2:
Cutting

Measure and mark all pieces on plywood. Make rough cuts 1 and 2 (indicated by circled numbers) to separate plywood into manageable pieces, with cutting guide clamped in place to assure straight cuts. Cut all pieces, with cutting guide clamped in place.

NOTE: For cutting angle cuts, lay out with T-bevel and mark carefully. Draw the Back and two Legs to full scale on your working surface. Assemble Legs to Back (see below) and lay down on top of drawing to make sure angle is correct. If angle differs, adjust Seat Brace to fit before cutting.

Using router and ¾" straight bit (or size to fit plywood width), make 1/16" deep

Materials

1 - 4'x8' sheet ¾" cabinet grade birch veneer plywood
2 - 6' lengths piano hinge
1 quart polyurethane varnish
Turpentine or paint thinner
Sandpaper, fine/80 grit
Fine steel wool

Tools

Electric circular saw with hollow ground plywood blade
Saber saw, for cutting curved seat
Hack saw, for cutting hinges
Combination square, for measuring and marking
Router with ¾" straight bit, for making slot that fixes chair in open position
Compass or string and pencil, for marking curved seat
Awl or ice pick
Screwdriver appropriate for screws that come with piano hinges
Cutting guide, 6'

Materials

1 - 4'x8' sheet ¾" cabinet grade birch veneer plywood
2 - 6' lengths piano hinge
¼" dowel
Polyurethane varnish
Turpentine or paint thinner
Sandpaper, fine/80 grit
Fine steel wool
Oil base enamel in color of choice

Tools

Electric circular saw with hollow
  ground plywood blade
Electric variable speed drill with ¼"
  auger-type bit, and hole-cutting saw
  or 1½" auger-type bit
Saber saw
Router with ¾" straight bit or size to fit
  plywood width
Hack saw, for cutting piano hinges
Awl or ice pick
Screwdriver appropriate to screws that
  come with piano hinges
T-bevel, for marking angles
Cutting guide, 4'

dado groove in each Leg where shown in Cutting Diagram. Using hack saw, cut hinges to fit dimensions of Seat, Seat Brace, and Legs. **NOTE:** Piano hinges come with pre-drilled holes 2 inches apart; cut hinges exactly between holes for ease of handling.

Assembly

NOTE: It is advisable to fully assemble one chair before mass-producing others.

Set Legs end-to-end and hinge together, using awl or ice pick to start screw holes. Hinge back Leg to Back at floor level. Lay assembly on top of full scale drawing to determine exact angles for Seat Brace. Cut Seat Brace, using saber saw for correct angles and hole-cutting saw for curve that fits over Legs (see Assembly Diagram 1-A).

Using awl or ice pick to start screw holes, attach hinge to Seat Brace; attach Seat Brace to underside of Seat. Attach hinge to rear edge of Seat. Position Seat Brace in place on Legs and mark where Seat hinge hits the Back; attach Seat to Back.

Drill ¼" hole through Seat Brace and Front Leg. Cut dowel to length (approximately 4½"). Insert dowel in hole to lock Leg in open position (see Assembly Diagram 1-C).

Finishing

Using a mixture of 1 part turpentine or paint thinner to 3 parts polyurethane varnish, finish chair with three coats. Allow each coat to dry thoroughly. Lightly sand between coats, and buff lightly with steel wool after final coat. Paint routed groove with three coats of oil base enamel in color of your choice, sanding lightly between coats.

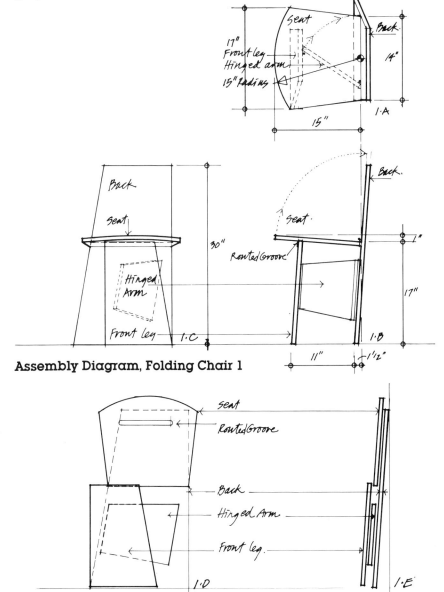

Assembly Diagram, Folding Chair 1

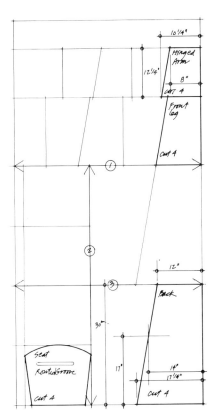

Cutting Diagram, Folding Chair 1

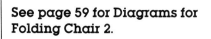

See page 59 for Diagrams for Folding Chair 2.

35

A Modern Chair with Old-Fashioned Comfort

A Modern Chair with Old-Fashioned Comfort

If you're tired of the same old stuffed style, here's a chance to create a truly modern look that's just right for you. This striking chair has the sleek, spare lines of today's high tech designs, yet the futon cushion makes it so inviting to sit down and relax. Plus, it's easy to build and it only takes one sheet of plywood for a pair! If you don't need another chair, use the same plans to make a loveseat couch . . . or use two plywood sheets to make a pair of chairs **and** a loveseat, for a beautifully coordinated set.

INSTRUCTIONS:

Cutting

NOTE: Two chairs or one loveseat can be cut from one sheet of plywood. Adjust widths of Seat, Back, and Seat Ledge to accommodate the sizes of your futon or cushions.

Measure and mark all pieces on plywood sheet. Make rough cuts 1 and 2 (indicated by circled numbers) to separate plywood into manageable pieces, with cutting guide clamped in place to assure straight cuts.

Mark and cut all pieces, with cutting guide clamped in place. Use compass or string and pencil to mark curved Sides; cut with saber saw. Cut dowels into 2½'' lengths.

Using router and ¾'' bit, make the dado grooves in the Sides (see Cutting Diagram).

Assembly

Glue and clamp Seat, Back, and Seat Ledge into routed slots. When glue is dry, drill holes from outside, approximately 2½'' deep and 3'' apart along glued joint. Apply glue to holes and dowels; tap dowels into holes. When dry, sand dowel ends until smooth and flush with surface.

Glue and clamp Arm Brace to underside of Arm. When glue is dry, dowel along glued joint from top side of Arm. Glue and clamp Arm to Side. When glue is dry, dowel along glued joint from inside. Sand all dowel ends until smooth and flush with surface.

Finishing

Using a mixture of 1 part turpentine or paint thinner to 3 parts polyurethane varnish, finish chairs with three coats. Allow each coat to dry thoroughly. Lightly sand between coats, and buff lightly with steel wool after final coat.

One-piece futon cushions can be custom made to the measurements of your chairs, or separate cushions for seat and back can be made in the shape and fabric of your choice.

For variation, make the Sides in different geometric shapes or design cutout shapes in the Sides and Back. Let your imagination flow if you'd rather not use a clear finish, and choose from painting in solid or speckled colors, stenciling, upholstering, or applying upholsterer's tacks like studs in a decorative design.

Materials

1 - 4'x8' sheet ¾'' cabinet grade birch veneer plywood
¼'' dowels
Futon or cushions to fit seat width
Waterproof wood glue
1 quart polyurethane varnish
Turpentine or paint thinner
Sandpaper, fine/80 grit
Fine steel wool

Tools

Electric circular saw with hollow ground plywood blade
Electric variable speed drill with ¼'' auger-type bit
Saber saw, to cut curved sides
Router with ¾'' straight bit or size to fit plywood
Bar clamps
Compass or string and pencil, for marking curved sides
Cutting guide, 4'

Futon cushions by Futon Designs, Asheville, North Carolina.

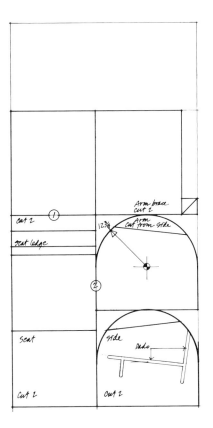

Cutting Diagram

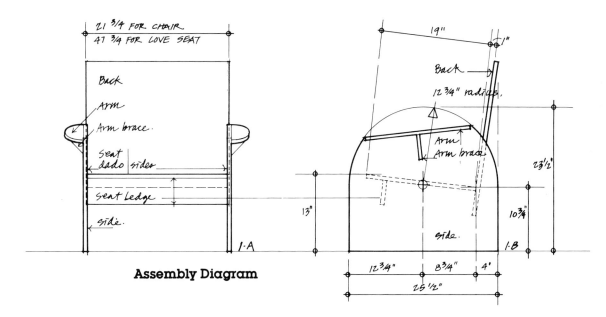

Assembly Diagram

A Stylish Trio For Any Home

41

A Stylish Trio For Any Home

For casual, at-home living, this ingenious project adds a special pizzazz. Making use of the wood's attractive grain, coupled with high gloss enamel paint, you can create a look that fits any decorating scheme. Add to its sleek design function plus— rearrange the units for a pair of sturdy benches, much-needed shelf space, or a unique occasional table for coffee or brunch.

INSTRUCTIONS:

Cutting

NOTE: Because the two loose inserts for Top C will receive a clear finish and will serve as part of the table top in certain configurations, it may be desirable to rearrange the cutting layout so these pieces are located on that area of the plywood that has the more interesting grain.

Measure and mark all pieces on plywood sheets. Make four rough cuts (indicated by circled numbers) to separate plywood into manageable pieces, with cutting guide clamped in place to assure straight cuts.

Use circular saw to make all cuts, with cutting guide clamped in place to assure straight and true cuts. Sand all edges and surfaces as necessary.

Assembly

To produce each of the four boxes required, glue and nail together with 8d nails two Side A pieces and two Side B pieces, as shown in Assembly Diagram 2-C. Set nails approximately 1/16" below the surface of the plywood.

Glue and nail Top A pieces to pairs of assembled boxes using 8d nails and setting them as above.

Fill all nail holes with wood filler and allow to dry; sand smooth. The nail holes should be invisible, so repeat the filling and sanding until the surface is completely smooth and flush. The first filling will require overnight drying; subsequent fillings will require 6-8 hours.

Finishing

Using a mixture of 3 parts polyurethane varnish and 1 part turpentine, seal assembled units and all other components with 3 coats. **NOTE:** All surfaces and all edges are to be sealed **except** those areas where glue is to be applied—Sides B, back surfaces of Sides C, Sides D, and Tops B (see Assembly Diagram 2). Allow each coat to dry and lightly sand between first and second coats. When third coat is dry, buff lightly with steel wool.

Apply first and second coats of First Color, as shown in Assembly Diagram 2, in the same way you sealed the units, leaving surfaces to receive glue unpainted and sanding lightly between coats. Check for nail holes that might still be visible at this point; fill, allow to dry, and sand smooth. Apply third coat of First Color and allow to dry thoroughly.

Glue Tops B, Sides C, and Sides D in place and nail with the 6d nails. Note that there is a ¾" painted reveal all around except where side pieces meet tops. Set nails approximately 1/16" below surface as before and fill. Fill also the cut ends of Tops B and the joints between Sides C and Tops B. Repeat until all filled joints, nail holes, and cut ends are flush and smooth.

Apply first and second coats of Second Color to Tops B, Sides C, and Sides D as shown in Assembly Diagram 2. Sand and fill as required between coats.

This handy trio can be arranged as a pair of benches, stacking shelves, or a Japanese-style low table. When the units are used as benches, simply store the two Top C pieces in a closet. When stacked as shelves, Top C pieces function as the middle shelves. For a coffee table, the Top C pieces fit perfectly as the central panel between the two benches. For greater leg room underneath the table, simply turn the Top C pieces sideways or perpendicular to the two benches—presto, you're ready to seat four for brunch.

Materials

3 - 4'x8' sheets ¾" cabinet grade birch veneer plywood
6d and 8d finishing nails
Oil-base gloss enamel paints
Polyurethane varnish
Turpentine or paint thinner
Waterproof wood glue
Wood filler
Sandpaper, fine/80 grit
Steel wool, fine

Tools

Electric circular saw with hollow ground plywood blade
C-clamps
Nail set
Cutting guide, 5'

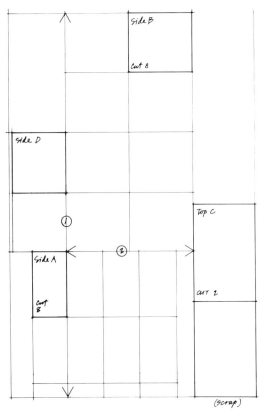

Cutting Diagram 1

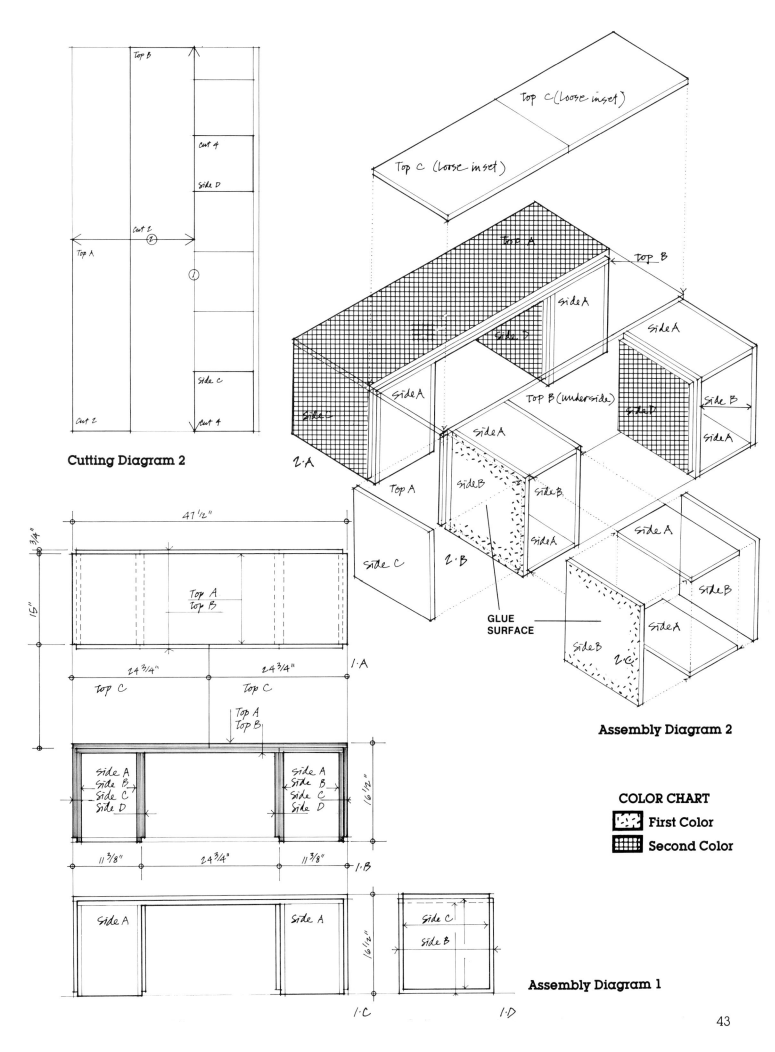

Cutting Diagram 2

Top B

cut 4

Side D

cut 2
②

Top A

①

Side c

cut 2

cut 4

Assembly Diagram 2

Top C (Loose inset)

Top C (Loose inset)

Top A

Top B

Side A

Side D

Side A

Side A

Side A

Top B (underside)

side D

Side B

Side A

Side C

2·A

Top A

Side B

Side B

Side C

2·B

Side A

Side A

GLUE SURFACE

Side B

Side A

Side B

2·C

Side B

COLOR CHART

First Color

Second Color

47 1/2"

3/4"

15"

Top A
Top B

24 3/4"

24 3/4"

1·A

Top C

Top C

Top A
Top B

Side A
Side B
Side C
Side D

Side A
Side B
Side C
Side D

16 1/2"

11 3/8"

24 3/4"

11 3/8"

1·B

Side A

Side A

16 1/2"

Side C

Side B

Assembly Diagram 1

1·C

1·D

43

Dining Tables Grow with Size of Guest List

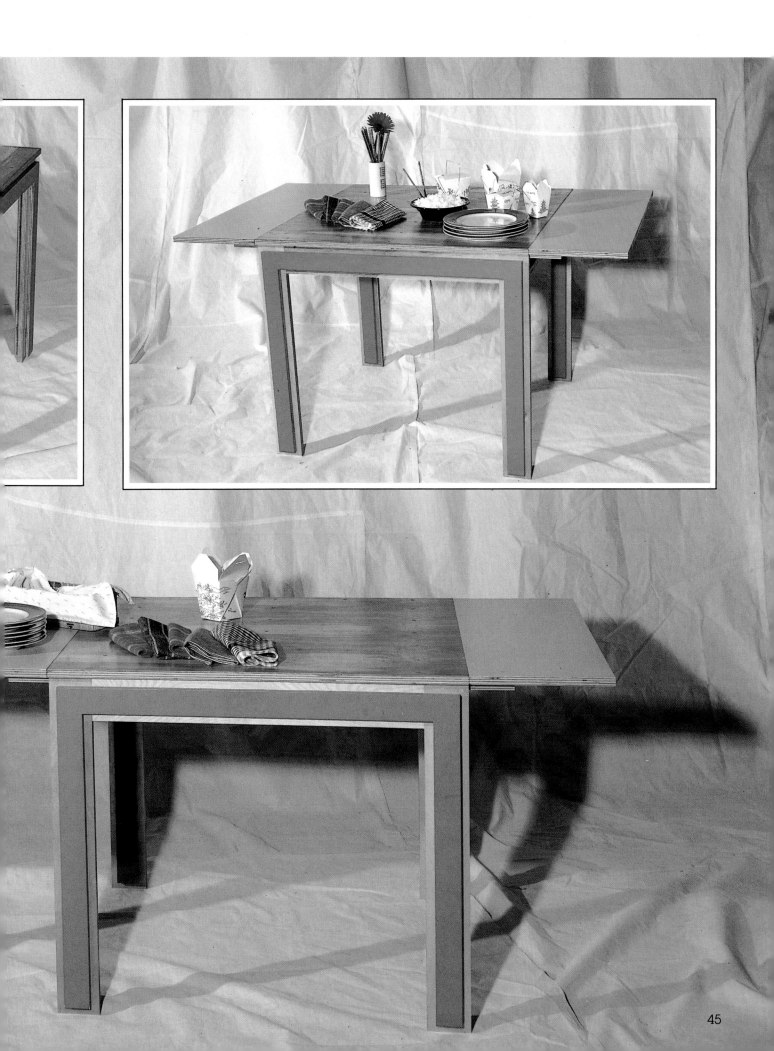

Dining Tables Grow with Size of Guest List

These dining tables expand or contract to fit the number of people you need to seat. And you don't have to worry about where to store the leaves—storage space is built right into the tables themselves! The individual 3x3 foot tables are perfect for small family meals, but when guests arrive put them together for a 10-foot long table that can handle a crowd.

INSTRUCTIONS:

Cutting and Assembly

Measure and mark all pieces on plywood. Make seven rough cuts (indicated by circled numbers) to separate plywood into manageable pieces, with cutting guides clamped in place to assure straight cuts.

Using table saw, rip all pieces for Legs and Leg Trim. Using circular saw or radial arm saw, cut Legs, Leg Trim, Cross Pieces, and Cross Piece Trim to length dimensions. Cut dowels into 2½" lengths.

Glue four Leg and Cross Piece units together; glue and nail Leg Trim to Legs and Cross Piece Trim to Cross Pieces. Set nails 1/16" below surface and fill nail holes with wood filler. When dry, sand until smooth and flush with surface.

Glue Spacer B pieces between pairs of Leg/Cross Piece units to form table base. Glue Spacer A pieces on table base, as shown in Assembly Diagram 1-B.

Cut Leaf Ledge (this piece supports stored leaves underneath the tabletop surface). Glue and nail Leaf Ledge to lower Spacer B (see Assembly Diagram 1-F).

Cut two Top Pieces apart and glue to top of table bases along Cross Pieces and Spacers A. Drill ¼" holes approximately 2½" deep and 6" apart along glued joints. Apply glue to holes and dowel lengths; tap dowels into holes. When dry, sand dowel ends until smooth and flush with surface. Trim outside edges of tabletops to fit bases evenly.

Cut two 12" Leaves and one 24" Leaf, following dimensions in Assembly Diagram 1-C. Cut Leaf Tabs, following dimensions in Assembly Diagram 1-C. Make sure Tabs will fit in slot when tabletop is in place; sand Tab down to fit so it will slide in and out of the slot, yet still be a tight fit. While Leaf Tab is positioned in slot, glue and nail Leaf to Leaf Tab from top side. Set nails and fill nail holes as above.

Finishing

Using oil base enamel in color of your choice, paint Leg Trim and Leaves with 3 coats, sanding lightly between coats. Using a mixture of 1 part turpentine or paint thinner and 3 parts polyurethane varnish, finish Leaf Tabs with one coat; when dry, rub Tabs with beeswax or bar soap to facilitate their fit into slots. Finish unpainted parts of Legs and tabletops with 3 coats, sanding lightly between coats and buffing with fine steel wool after the final coat.

Materials

2 - 4'x8' sheets plus scraps ¾" cabinet grade birch veneer plywood
¼" dowels
3d finishing nails
Waterproof wood glue
Wood filler
Polyurethane varnish
Turpentine or paint thinner
Sandpaper, fine/80 grit
Fine steel wool
Oil base enamel in color of choice

Tools

Table saw, for ripping lengths
Radial arm saw, for cross-cutting
Electric circular saw with hollow ground plywood blade
Electric variable speed drill with ¼" auger-type bit
Nail set
Bar clamps
Cutting guides, 4' and 8'

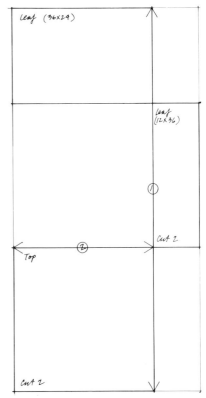

Cutting Diagram 1

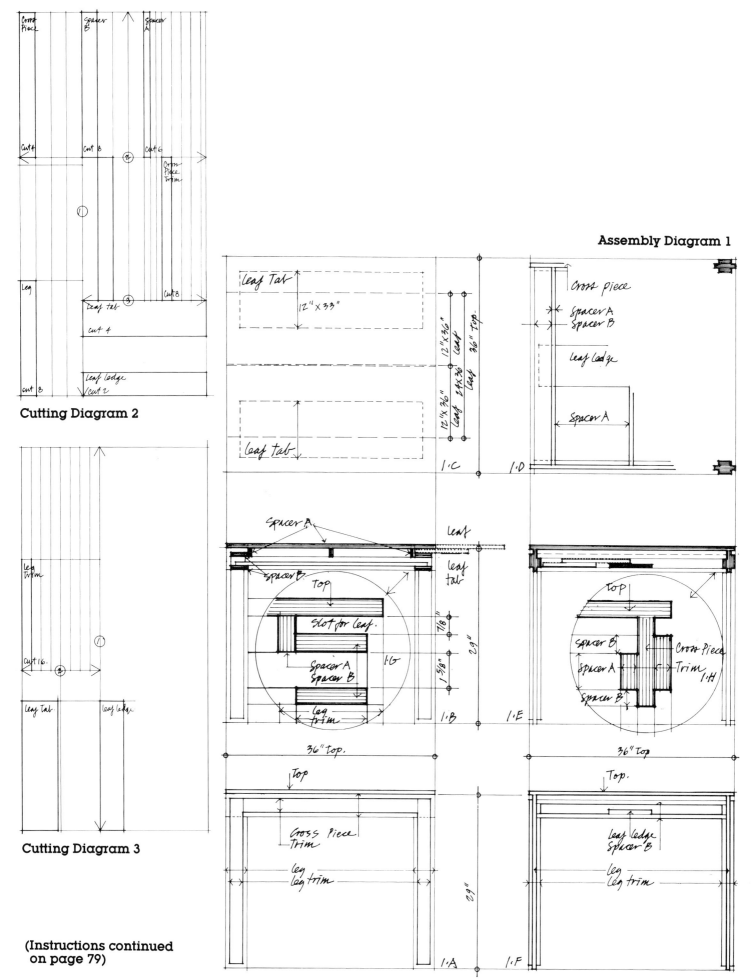

Cutting Diagram 2

Cutting Diagram 3

(Instructions continued on page 79)

Assembly Diagram 1

47

TV Trays Redefined for Today

Tripod Legs for Sturdy Support

TV Trays Redefined for Today

Nearly everyone will agree that TV trays can be indispensable, but are almost always unattractive, poorly made, or boring in design. Here's a trio of nesting tables, sized like standard TV tables, but far more interesting and versatile. They're doweled for sturdy construction and they stack neatly and quickly. Even without the TV, these nesting tables will soon become indispensable in your home.

INSTRUCTIONS:

Cutting

NOTE: Three nesting tables can be cut from one plywood sheet.

Measure and mark all pieces on plywood. Make three rough cuts (indicated by circled numbers) to separate plywood into manageable pieces, with cutting guide clamped in place to assure straight cuts. Cut all other pieces, with cutting guide clamped in place. Cut dowels into 2½" lengths.

Using router, make a ¼" deep dado groove along the entire length of each Side piece (see Cutting Diagram). Arrange a stop approximately 5¾" from bottom edge and make two more ¼" deep dado grooves up to the stop, to finish cutting the slot in the Sides.

Assembly

Line up Tops with Sides to make sure they fit exactly. Glue and clamp Tops to Sides. When glue is dry, drill ¼" holes approximately 2½" deep and 3" apart along glued joints. Apply glue to holes and dowel lengths; tap dowels into holes. When dry, sand dowel ends until smooth and flush with surface.

Slide Spacer into ¼" deep dado groove in Sides (see Assembly Diagram). Glue and dowel Spacer between Sides from the outside.

Finishing

Using a mixture of 1 part turpentine or paint thinner to 3 parts polyurethane varnish, finish tables with three coats. Allow each coat to dry thoroughly. Lightly sand between coats, and buff lightly with steel wool after final coat.

For design variation, paint Spacers with three coats of oil base enamel in color(s) of your choice, sanding lightly between coats. Paint the Tops or cover them with a plastic laminate surface.

Materials

1 - 4'x8' sheet ¾" cabinet grade birch veneer plywood
¼" dowels
Waterproof wood glue
1 quart polyurethane varnish
Turpentine or paint thinner
Sandpaper, fine/80 grit
Fine steel wool

Tools

Electric circular saw with hollow ground plywood blade
Electric variable speed drill with ¼" auger-type bit
Saber saw
Router with ¾" straight bit, or size to fit plywood width
Bar clamps
Cutting guide, 4'

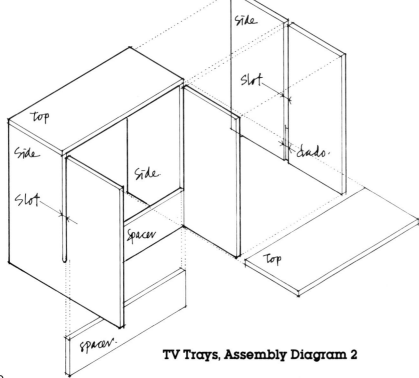

TV Trays, Assembly Diagram 2

Cutting Diagram

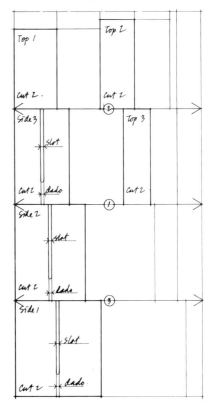

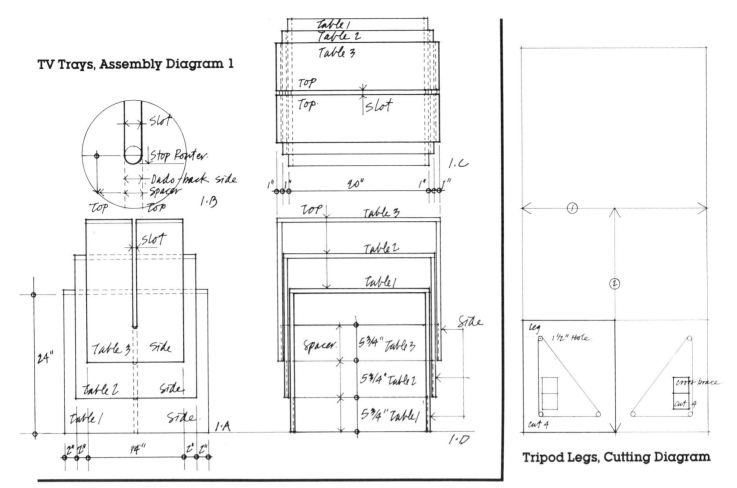

TV Trays, Assembly Diagram 1

Tripod Legs, Cutting Diagram

Tripod Legs for Sturdy Support

For a new twist in sawhorses, these triangular legs give sturdy support for any surface—butcher block table, slick melamine desktop, glass top coffee table. They're built to take the weight, but are lightweight themselves and easy to build. They fold up instantly for easy storage, but are attractive enough to leave them showing all the time. With a spot of accent color, these great sawhorse legs make any topping special.

Materials

1 - 4'x8' sheet ¾" cabinet grade birch veneer plywood
1 - 6' length piano hinge
1 quart polyurethane varnish
Turpentine or paint thinner
Sandpaper, fine/80 grit
Fine steel wool
Oil base enamel paint, in color of your choice

INSTRUCTIONS:
Cutting

NOTE: One pair of sawhorse legs can be cut out of 2/3 sheet of plywood; three pair can be cut out of two sheets of plywood.

Measure and mark all pieces on plywood. Make two rough cuts (indicated by circled numbers) to separate plywood into manageable pieces, with cutting guide clamped in place to assure straight cuts.

Drill 1½" holes where shown; holes can be geometric design of your choice.
NOTE: When drilling holes, make certain the back side of the plywood is in contact with a flat piece of scrap board. Move the scrap board between drillings for a fresh flat surface. This prevents splintering of the plywood face.

Connect the outside circumferences of the three drilled holes, to make a triangle. Using saber saw, cut out triangular shape (see Cutting Diagram).

Cut out hinged Cross Braces (each pair of Legs has one hinged Cross Brace).

Cut hinges to fit Leg and Cross Brace dimensions. **NOTE:** Piano hinges come with pre-drilled holes 2 inches apart; cut hinges exactly between holes for ease of handling.

(Instructions continued on page 63)

Tables Set for High Tea

Tables Set for High Tea

When you're ready for a quiet break in the busy day, take advantage of tea time and set up these attractive tables for an invigorating snack and a few moments of peace. Designed for simple good looks, these easy-to-build tables are accented with a touch of bright color. When tea time is over, get ready for breakfast, brunch, or a quiet dinner for two.

INSTRUCTIONS:

Cutting and Assembly

NOTE: Select plywood grain for table Top so that it runs continuously across the surface.

Measure and mark all pieces on plywood. Make three rough cuts (indicated by circled numbers) to separate plywood into manageable pieces, with cutting guide clamped in place to assure straight cuts. Using table saw, rip all pieces for Legs, Leg Trim, and Cross Braces, following dimensions in Assembly Diagram 1. Reset table saw to bevel edges of Leg Trim.

Using circular saw or radial arm saw, cut Legs, Leg Trim, and Cross Braces to length dimensions. **NOTE:** When cutting repetitive pieces the same length, arrange some kind of stop or block at the end of each cut so that all pieces will be identical lengths. Bevel cut bottom edge of Leg Trim, as shown in Assembly Diagram 1-A. Cut dowels into 2½" lengths.

Using saber saw, cut slots in Cross Braces, where shown in Cutting Diagram. Position Legs and Cross Braces as shown in Assembly Diagram 2. Glue together at corners. Glue and nail Leg Trim to Legs. Set nails 1/16" below surface and fill holes with wood filler. When dry, sand until smooth and flush with surface. Assemble Leg/Cross Brace units perpendicularly, to form base of table.

If using plywood sheet instead of scraps, cut two table Tops apart. Make four Top cuts and glue in place on table Base, making sure grain is continuous across surface. Drill ¼" holes approximately 2½" deep and 6" apart along joints (see Assembly Diagram 2-B). Apply glue to holes and to dowel lengths; tap dowels into holes. When dry, sand dowel ends until smooth and flush with surface. **NOTE:** In the table shown here, 5/16" dowels were used in combination with the ¼" dowels for a decorative effect. Trim outside edges of table to form an even square.

Finishing

Check all nail holes to make sure they are completely smooth and flush with surface; sand if necessary. Using oil base enamel in color of your choice, paint Leg Trim with 3 coats, sanding lightly between coats.

Using a mixture of 1 part turpentine or paint thinner and 3 parts polyurethane varnish, finish all unpainted plywood with 3 coats, sanding lightly between coats and buffing with fine steel wool after the final coat.

Materials

Plywood scraps, or 1 - 4'x8' sheet ¾" cabinet grade birch veneer plywood for two tables
3d finishing nails
Wood filler
¼" dowels
Waterproof wood glue
Polyurethane varnish
Turpentine or paint thinner
Sandpaper, fine/80 grit
Fine steel wool
Oil base enamel in color of choice

Tools

Table saw, for ripping lengths
Electric circular saw with hollow ground plywood blade
Saber saw
Electric variable speed drill with ¼" auger-type bit
Nail set
Bar clamps
Cutting guide, 6'

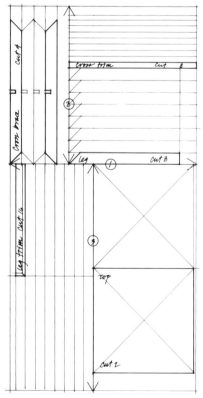

Cutting Diagram

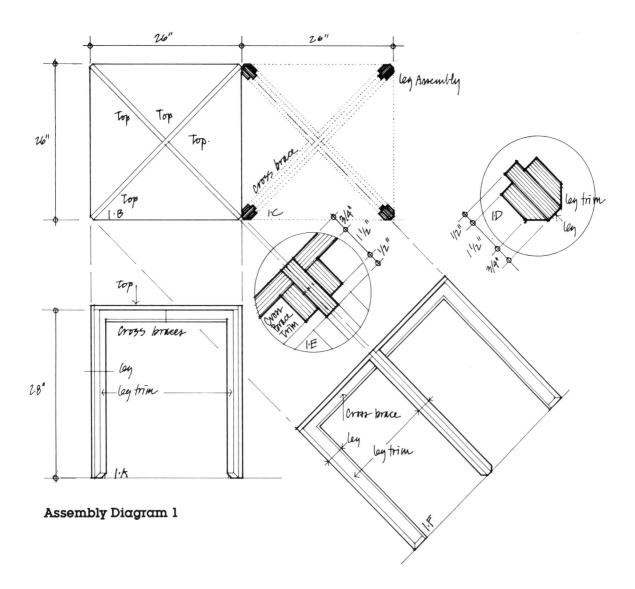

26"   26"

26"

Top   Top
        Top.
Top
1·B   1·C

Leg Assembly

3/4"
1 1/2"
1/2"

Cross brace trim
1·E

Leg trim
Leg
1/2"   1 1/2"   3/4"
1·D

Top

Cross braces

Leg
Leg trim

28"

1·A

Cross brace
Leg
Leg trim
1·F

Assembly Diagram 1

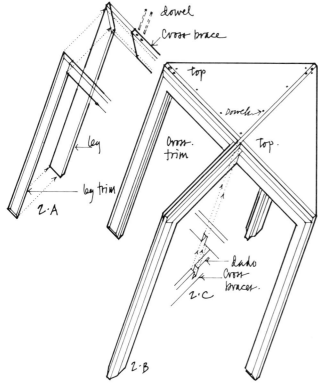

dowel
Cross brace

top

Leg

dowel

Cross
trim

Top.

Leg trim

2·A

Cross braces
dado

2·C

2·B

Assembly Diagram 2

A New Angle on Stacking Tables

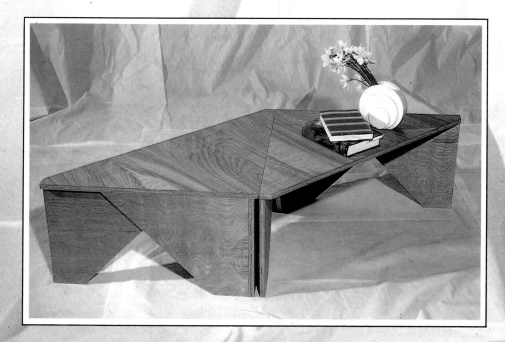

A New Angle on Stacking Tables

This quartet of stacking tables is a space saver as well as a fresh interpretation of a classic idea. Each individual unit has a myriad of occasional uses, but put them all together for a distinctive coffee table or arrange them in pairs for convenient end tables. When you don't need them, just stack them up — they're built to fit perfectly in any corner.

INSTRUCTIONS:

Cutting

NOTE: Four nesting tables can be cut from one plywood sheet. To take advantage of the wood's attractive grain in a continuous pattern when the four tables are assembled as one, rearrange the cutting layout to suit plywood.

Measure and mark all pieces on plywood. Make rough cuts 1 and 2 (indicated by circled numbers) to separate plywood into manageable pieces, with cutting guide clamped in place to assure straight cuts. **NOTE:** Rectangular Leg pieces are cut in half diagonally to form individual Legs. Cut ¼" dowels into 2½" lengths.

Assembly

Invert one Leg piece and place over another Leg piece to make the Leg assembly. Glue and clamp triangular overlap (see Assembly Diagram 2); when dry, drill ¼" holes approximately 2½" deep at three corners of triangular overlap. Apply glue to holes and to dowel lengths; tap dowels into holes. When dry, sand dowel ends until smooth and flush with surface.

Glue and clamp pairs of Leg assemblies together at 90° angles to make the table bases. Glue and dowel as above, along corners.

Glue and clamp Tops onto bases; glue and dowel as above, along edges. Trim outside edges of Tops evenly.

Finishing

Using a mixture of 1 part turpentine or paint thinner to 3 parts polyurethane varnish, finish tables with three coats. Allow each coat to dry thoroughly. Lightly sand between coats, and buff lightly with steel wool after final coat.

Materials

1 - 4'x8' sheet ¾" cabinet grade birch veneer plywood
¼" dowels
3d finishing nails
Wood putty
Waterproof wood glue
1 quart polyurethane varnish
Turpentine or paint thinner
Sandpaper, fine/80 grit
Fine steel wool
Oil base enamel paint in color of your choice

Tools

Electric circular saw with hollow ground plywood blade
Electric variable speed drill with ¼" auger-type bit
Nail set
Bar clamps
Cutting guide, 4'

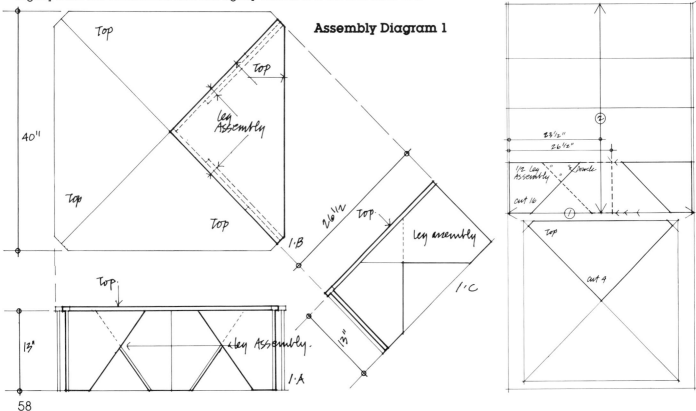

Assembly Diagram 1

Cutting Diagram

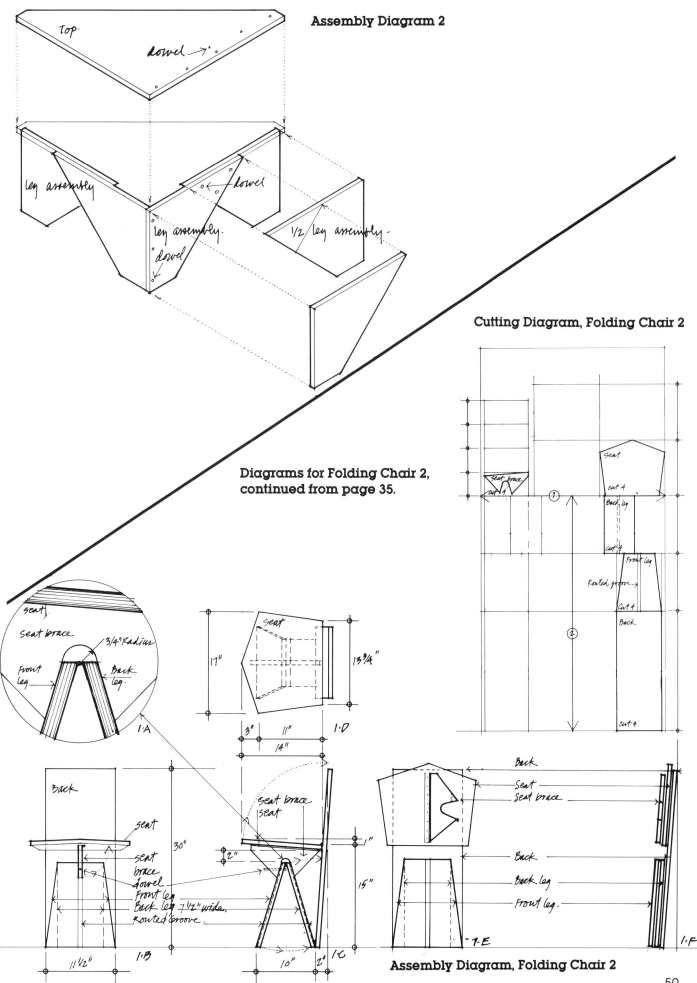

Assembly Diagram 2

Top.

dowel →

leg assembly

dowel

leg assembly.

dowel

1/2 leg assembly.

Cutting Diagram, Folding Chair 2

Seat brace
cut 4

Seat
cut 4

Back leg
cut 4

Front leg

Routed groove →

Cut 4

Back

cut 4

①

②

**Diagrams for Folding Chair 2,
continued from page 35.**

seat

Seat brace

Front
leg →

3/4" Radius

Back
leg.

1·A

Seat

17"

13 3/4"

3"   11"
14"

1·D

Seat brace
seat

30"

Back

seat

seat
brace
dowel
Front leg
Back leg 7 1/2" wide.
Routed groove.

1·B

11 1/2"

2"

15"

1"

1·C

10"   2"

Back

Seat
Seat brace

Back

Back leg

Front leg.

~ 1·E

1·F

Assembly Diagram, Folding Chair 2

A Healthy Serving of High Style

A Healthy Serving of High Style

When you don't want to sacrifice good looks for foldability, this hinged table is a beautiful option. Its two sides fold down in a second, for easy, out-of-the-way storage, and the handy shelves are a perfect place for your serving bowls, cookbooks, and accessories. Open out one or both hinged sides and you have a comfortable table for a buffet or sit-down affair, with soup bowls and dessert plates ready and waiting on the built-in shelves.

INSTRUCTIONS:

Cutting

NOTE: If you decide to take advantage of the wood's attractive grain in the three top pieces, rearranging of the cutting layout may require a second sheet of plywood for the other pieces.

Measure and mark all pieces on plywood. Make three rough cuts (indicated by circled numbers) to separate plywood into manageable pieces, with 8' cutting guide clamped in place to assure straight cuts. **NOTE:** Do not cut three Top pieces apart until after slots for Table Base have been cut in underside of Fixed Top; after determining that Fixed Top will fit onto Base exactly, cut off hinged portions.

Measure and mark all other pieces, with 4' cutting guide clamped in place. Cut dowels into 2½" lengths. Cut hinges, to fit dimensions of Hinged Tops and Legs. **NOTE:** Piano hinges come with pre-drilled holes 2 inches apart; cut hinges exactly between holes for ease of handling.

Assembly

Using router, make dado grooves in Sides for Shelves and Base Divider. Apply glue into slots, place Shelves and Base Divider into slots, and clamp. When glue is dry, drill ¼" holes approximately 2½" deep and 6" apart, along glued joints. Apply glue to holes and to cut dowels; tap dowels into holes. When glue is dry, sand dowels until smooth and flush with surface. Clamp, glue, and dowel Base between Sides in same manner.

Make dado grooves in Fixed Top; once it is determined that Fixed Top correctly fits on the Table Base, cut off hinged portions of Top. Glue slots, apply Top to Table Base, and clamp. When glue is dry, drill ¼" holes approximately 2½" deep and 6" apart. Apply glue to holes and to cut dowels; tap dowels into holes. When glue is dry, sand dowels until smooth and flush with Fixed Top surface.

Using awl or ice pick to start screw holes, attach two Hinged Tops to each side of center Fixed Top. Attach hinges to edges of Legs; hinge Legs to Table Base.

Using router, make dado groove in Stop. Open Leg to full open position, to determine location for Stop (Stop fixes Leg in open position). Apply Stop to underside of each Hinged Top with screws, nail, or glue.

Finishing

Using a mixture of 1 part turpentine or paint thinner to 3 parts polyurethane varnish, finish table with three coats. Allow each coat to dry thoroughly. Lightly sand between coats, and buff lightly with steel wool after final coat.

The table shown here was finished with clear polyurethane varnish to preserve the attractive grain that spreads continuously across the three Top pieces. Other options include painting the Top, the Legs, or the entire table with an oil base enamel paint in the color of your choice. Additionally, the tabletop can be covered with a plastic laminate surface.

Attach adjustable coasters to underside of each corner of Table Base and each Leg. Adjust until table is level. Coasters will also keep table from sliding.

Materials

1 - 4'x8' sheet ¾" cabinet grade birch veneer plywood
¼" dowels
2 - 6' lengths piano hinge
Waterproof wood glue
1 quart polyurethane varnish
Turpentine or paint thinner
Sandpaper, fine/80 grit
Fine steel wool
Adjustable coasters

Tools

Electric circular saw with hollow ground plywood blade
Electric variable speed drill with ¼" auger-type bit
Router with ¾" straight bit or size to fit plywood, for cutting dado grooves
Hack saw, for cutting piano hinges
Bar clamps
Awl or ice pick
Screwdriver appropriate for screws that come with piano hinges
Cutting guides, 4' and 8'

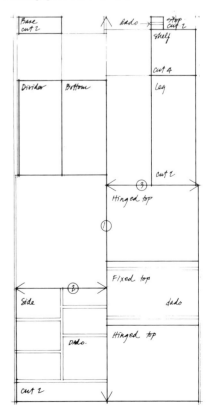

Cutting Diagram

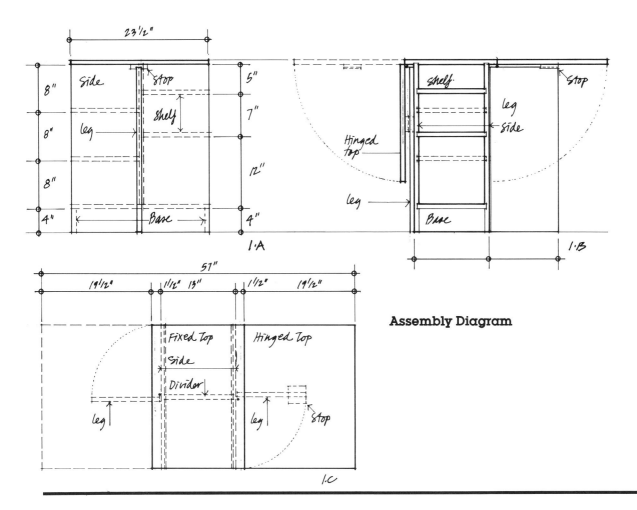

Assembly Diagram

Instructions for Tripod Legs, continued from page 51.

Tools

Electric circular saw with hollow
ground plywood blade
Electric variable speed drill with 1½"
auger-type bit
Saber saw, for cutting out triangle
Hack saw, for cutting piano hinges
Router with bit that cuts a ⅜" round, for
rounding off edges
Combination square, for laying out
cuts
Awl or ice pick
Screwdriver appropriate for screws
that come with piano hinges
Cutting guide, 4'

Assembly

Using awl or ice pick to start screw holes, hinge pairs of Cross Brace pieces together. Mark all other hinge locations, following Assembly Diagram 1-B. Lay each pair of Legs end to end; attach hinges to Legs. Attach hinges to outside edges of hinged Cross Braces; attach each edge of hinged Cross Brace to its matching Leg (remove screws from center hinge to facilitate access).

Use router to round off edges of Legs, as shown in Assembly Diagrams 1-C and 1-D.

Finishing

Using a mixture of 1 part turpentine or paint thinner to 3 parts polyurethane varnish, finish sawhorse legs with three coats. Allow each coat to dry thoroughly. Lightly sand between coats, and buff lightly with steel wool after final coat. Paint hinged Cross Braces with three coats of accent color of your choice, sanding lightly between first two coats.

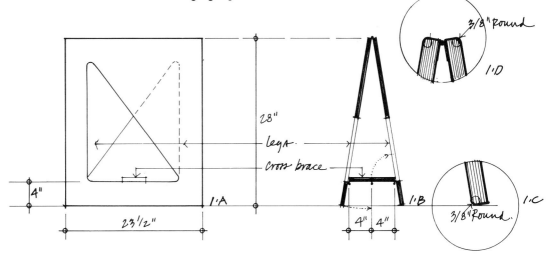

Assembly Diagram

Triad Legs for Shelf or Desk

Triad Legs for Shelf or Desk

These snappy triangle supports are unusual in their design—lightweight in look but heavyweight in their ability to support any type of tabletop surface. Easy to build, make them for a narrow behind-the-couch shelf to hold lamps and magazines, or make them taller for a desk or drafting table. Easy to make, easy to move, easy to adapt to all your needs!

INSTRUCTIONS:

Cutting

NOTE: It is recommended, to use up plywood scraps, to cut the Triad Legs from scraps and to use other lightweight tops for desk or shelf surfaces. However, all Legs and Tops for a 30"x60" desk and a 10"x84" magazine shelf can be cut from one plywood sheet.

Measure and mark all pieces on plywood. Make four rough cuts (indicated by circled numbers) to separate plywood into manageable pieces, with cutting guides clamped in place to assure straight cuts. Cut all pieces, with cutting guides clamped in place. **NOTE:** Cutting Legs will be easier if you use a table saw or radial arm saw. When cutting repetitive pieces the same length, regardless of the type of saw, arrange some kind of stop or block at the end of each cut so that all pieces will be identical lengths.

Using compass or circle template, mark curved ends of Legs, Bottoms, and Support; cut curved ends with saber saw or band saw.

Assembly

Mark location of drill holes in all curved ends; drill 1⅝" holes through ends. **NOTE:** When drilling holes, make certain the back side of the plywood is in contact with a flat piece of scrap board. Move the scrap board between drillings for a fresh flat surface. This prevents splintering of the plywood face. Cut 1⅝" dowels to length and insert in drilled holes to form triangular shape.

If the top surface is cut from plywood, it must be glued and doweled (¼" dowels) to the Shelf/Desk Support in several places to add stability (see Assembly Diagrams 1-B and 1-C). Use router to round off all edges of Shelf/Desk top surface.

Finishing

Using a mixture of 1 part turpentine or paint thinner to 3 parts polyurethane varnish, finish Legs with three coats. Allow each coat to dry thoroughly. Lightly sand between coats, and buff lightly with steel wool after final coat.

Materials

Assorted plywood scraps, for Legs only
    OR
1 - 4'x8' sheet ¾" cabinet grade birch veneer plywood, for Legs and Tops
¼" and 1⅝" dowels
Waterproof wood glue
1 quart polyurethane varnish
Turpentine or paint thinner
Sandpaper, fine/80 grit
Fine steel wool

Tools

Electric circular saw with hollow ground plywood blade
Electric variable speed drill with ¼" and 1⅝" auger-type bits
Saber saw
Router with bit that cuts a ⅜" round, for rounding off tabletop edges
Compass or circle template, for marking curved ends
Cutting guides, 4' and 8'

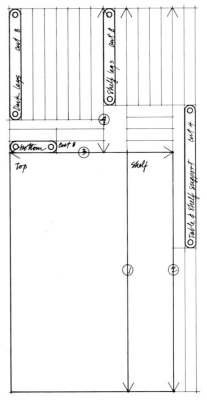

Cutting Diagram

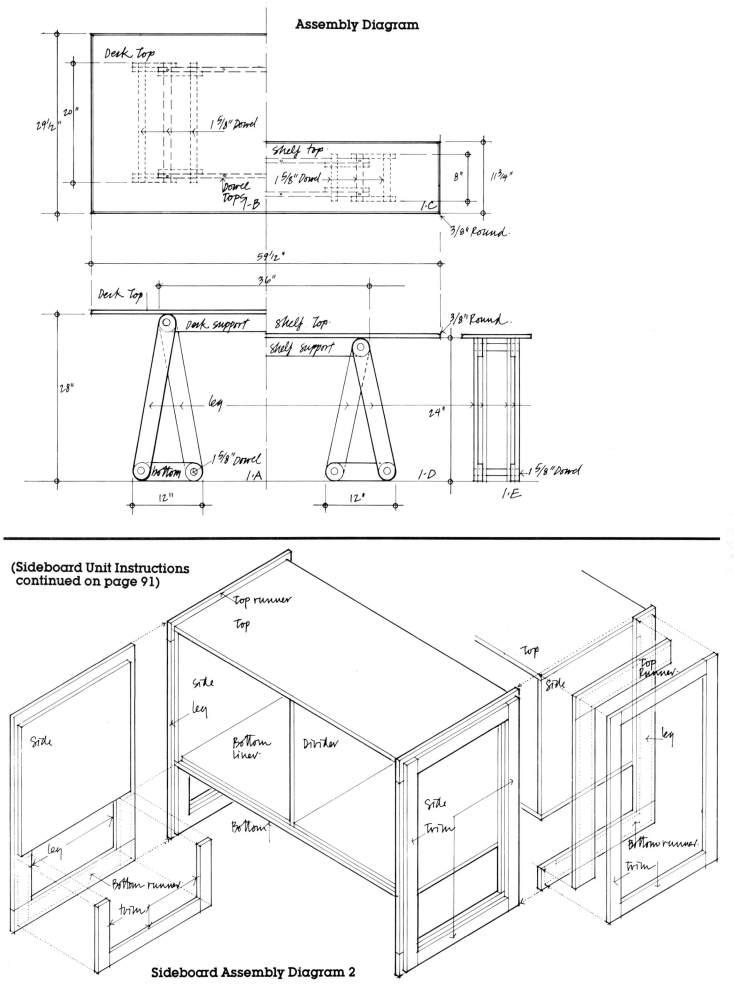

Assembly Diagram

Desk Top

29½" 20"

1 5/8" Dowel

Dowel Tops 1·B

shelf top

1 5/8" Dowel

8" 11¾"

1·C

3/8" Round.

59½"

36"

Desk Top

Desk support shelf Top.

3/8" Round.

shelf support

28"

leg

24"

Bottom 1 5/8" Dowel

12" 1·A

12' 1·D

1 5/8" Dowel

1·E

(Sideboard Unit Instructions continued on page 91)

Top runner

Top

Side

leg

Side

Bottom liner. Divider

Top

Side

Top Runner.

leg

Side Trim

Bottom

leg

Bottom runner

trim

Bottom runner

trim

Sideboard Assembly Diagram 2

A Drafting Table That Adjusts with Ease

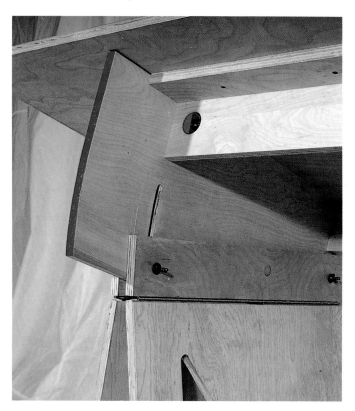

A Drafting Table That Adjusts with Ease

Everyone dreams of having a drafting table—a broad expanse of working surface that isn't cluttered with the knick-knacks that collect on a kitchen table. Here's an easy-to-build drafting table that adjusts to whatever tilt makes you comfortable. Whether you need it for drafting, drawing, needlecrafts, or as a study center, this table's good design will spark your own creative energy. Its good-looking legs are also sturdy support for any tabletop surface you choose.

INSTRUCTIONS:

Cutting

NOTE: Drafting table shown here uses a 3'x6' piece of plywood for its tabletop surface. A 3'x6'8" solid core door may also be used for tabletop. Standard drafting table height is 36 inches; all dimensions will need to be adjusted if table height is changed.

Measure and mark all pieces on plywood. Make rough cuts 1 and 2 (indicated by circled numbers) to separate plywood into manageable pieces, with cutting guide clamped in place to assure straight cuts. Mark and cut all other pieces, with cutting guide clamped in place.

Drill 1½" holes in Legs, where shown in Cutting Diagram. **NOTE:** When drilling holes, make certain the back side of the plywood is in contact with a flat piece of scrap board. Move the scrap board between drillings for a fresh flat surface. This prevents splintering of the plywood face. Connect the outside circumferences of the three drilled holes in each Leg, to make a triangle. Using saber saw, cut out triangular shape.

Using compass or string and pencil to assure smooth curve, mark curved arc of Tilting Arm's edge and curved slot in Tilting Arm, following Cutting Diagram. With saber saw, cut curved edge. Drill ⅜" holes where shown and use saber saw to cut out curved slot.

Cut hinges to fit Cross Brace and Leg dimensions. **NOTE:** Piano hinges come with pre-drilled holes 2 inches apart; cut hinges exactly between holes for ease of handling.

Assembly

Using awl or ice pick to start screw holes, hinge pairs of Cross Brace pieces together; attach hinges to outside edges of Hinged Cross Braces. Attach each edge of Hinged Cross Brace to its matching Leg (remove screws from center hinge to facilitate access).

For ease of handling, temporarily separate Cross Bars with a scrap piece of plywood the same thickness as the Tilting Arm; drill ¼" holes as shown in Assembly Diagram 1-A and 1-B, and bolt plywood scrap sandwiched between Cross Bars. Hinge a Leg to each Cross Bar (see Assembly Diagram 1-B).

Remove temporary spacers from Cross Bars and install Tilting Arm in down or flat position (see Assembly Diagram 1-B).

Drill 1½" holes through each end of Top Stiffener, where shown in Cutting Diagram. Drill ¼" holes through lengths of dowels or handrails, for the spacers between the Top Stiffener and wing nuts (see Assembly Diagram 1-C). Using oil base enamel paint in color of your choice, paint spacers with three coats, sanding lightly between coats.

Drill 5/16" holes through edges of Top Stiffener, for the bolts that go into the spacers. Screw Top Stiffener to underside of tabletop.

Place tabletop on Leg Assemblies; mark where drilled holes in edges of Top Stiffener meet Tilting Arm. Drill 5/16" holes in Tilting Arm (see Assembly Diagram 1-C). Insert bolts through Tilting Arm, Top Stiffener, and spacers; attach washers and wing nuts. To adjust the tilt of the tabletop, loosen bolts in curved slots, raise tabletop to desired angle and tighten down bolts.

Materials

1 - 4'x8' sheet ¾" cabinet grade birch veneer plywood
1 - 3'x6' piece ¾" cabinet grade birch veneer plywood, for tabletop
1 - 6' length piano hinge
1½" dowels, or length of handrail, ripped to half-rounds
8 - ¼"x3" elevator bolts (available through specialty nut and bolt companies)
8 wing nuts with washers, to fit elevator bolts
1½" x #6 flathead wood screws
1 quart polyurethane varnish
Turpentine or paint thinner
Sandpaper, fine/80 grit
Fine steel wool
Oil base enamel paint, in color of your choice

Tools

Electric circular saw with hollow ground plywood blade
Electric variable speed drill with adjustable auger-type bit
Saber saw, for cutting out triangular shape and curved slot
Hack saw, for cutting piano hinges
Combination square, for laying out cuts
Compass or string and pencil, for marking curves on tilting arm
Awl or ice pick
Screwdriver appropriate for screws that come with piano hinges
Cutting guide, 4'

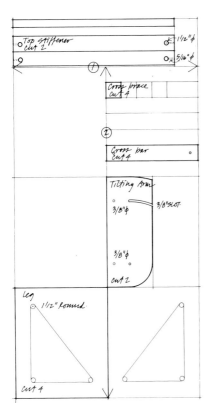

Finishing

Using a mixture of 1 part turpentine or paint thinner to 3 parts polyurethane varnish, finish legs with three coats. Allow each coat to dry thoroughly. Lightly sand between coats, and buff lightly with steel wool after final coat. Paint Hinged Cross Braces and edges of Tilting Arm with three coats of accent color of your choice, sanding lightly between first two coats.

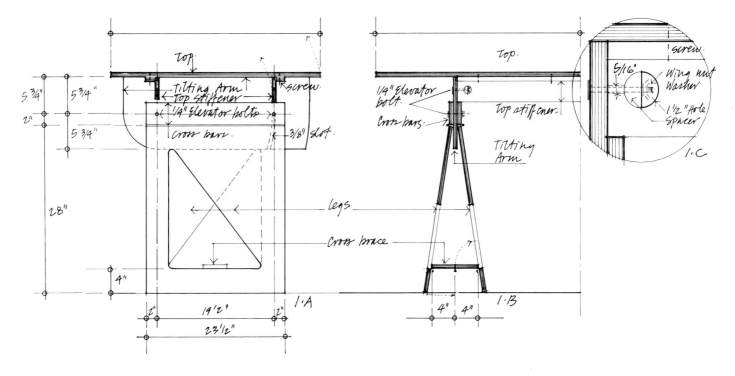

Assembly Diagram

3. Everything In Its Place . . .

A Cabinet with Dressed Up Style

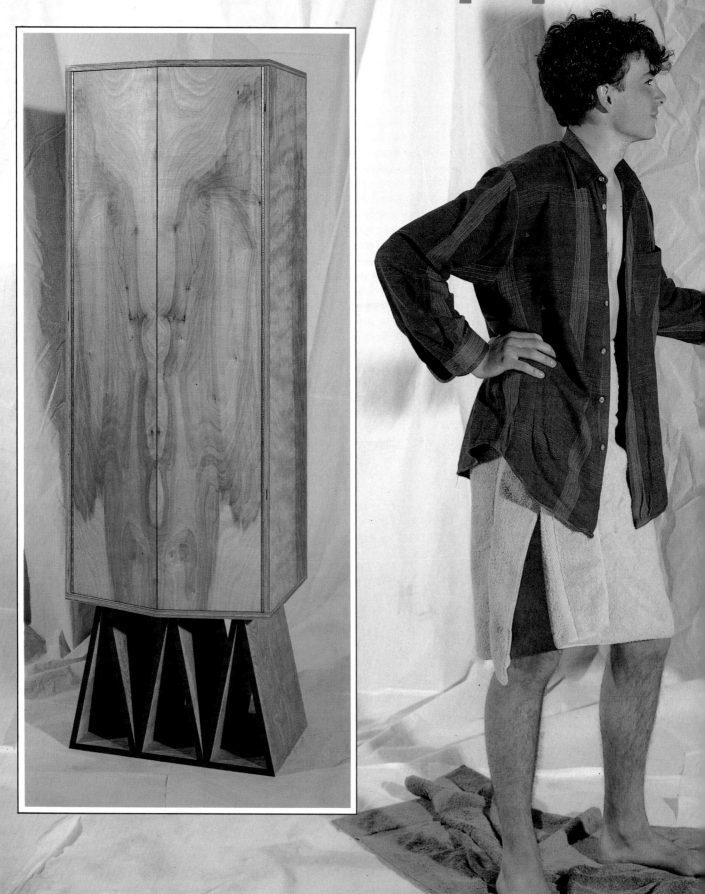

A Cabinet with Dressed Up Style

Here's a dramatically elegant way to store your own haute couture—from denims and oxford shirts to silk blouses and fine knits. This wardrobe unit takes advantage of the plywood's grain for a captivating effect. Its unusual base is a simple construction of A-frame components that can be easily expanded to any width desired. This special cabinet makes getting dressed a truly fashionable act.

INSTRUCTIONS:

Cutting

NOTE: Dimensions of cabinet shown here were determined by the plywood's attractive grain. Cabinet can be made wider, narrower, or shorter, depending on grain of wood and individual taste.

Measure and mark all pieces on plywood. Make six rough cuts (indicated by circled numbers) to separate plywood into manageable pieces, with cutting guide clamped in place to assure straight cuts.

Mark and cut all pieces for Base Assembly. Bevel cut edges as shown, to form correct angles when Base is assembled. Cut dowels into 2½" lengths. Using hack saw, cut piano hinges to fit dimensions of doors. **NOTE:** Piano hinges come with pre-drilled holes 2 inches apart; cut hinges exactly between holes for ease of handling.

Base Assembly

Lay Base Legs upright on work surface at the correct angles. Glue and screw Base Top and Base Bottom to Base Legs.

Cabinet Assembly

Glue and clamp Sides to Back. Drill ¼" holes approximately 2½" deep and 6" apart along glued joint. Apply glue to holes and dowel lengths; tap dowels into holes. When dry, sand dowel ends until smooth and flush with surface. Glue and dowel Top and Bottom to Sides/Back as above. Measure internal dimensions and cut Top and Bottom Liners to fit. Glue these pieces to Top and Bottom.

Cut Shelf Supports to length. Using router and full ¾" straight bit, make ¼"-deep dado grooves for Shelves. Glue and nail Shelf Supports to Sides. Set nails 1/16" below surface and fill holes with wood filler. When dry, sand until smooth and flush with surface.

Measuring from dado groove to dado groove, determine width of Shelves. Cut Shelves ⅛" less than measured dimension and set aside.

Cut Doors and using awl or ice pick to start screw holes, attach hinges to Doors. Attach door catch and knobs, and set aside.

Finishing

Remove hinges, door knobs, and door catch from Doors. Using a mixture of 1 part turpentine or paint thinner to 3 parts polyurethane varnish, finish with 3 coats, sanding lightly between coats and buffing with fine steel wool after the final coat. Paint facing edges of Base with three coats of oil base enamel in color of your choice. Put hardware back on Doors, mount Doors on front; slide Shelves into dado grooves.

Vary the design by adding A-frame units to widen the base for a wider cabinet. Or add a center divider and install shelves on one side and a hanging rod on the other. Install drawers instead of shelves, and vary the height of shelf openings for different sizes.

Materials

3 - 4'x8' sheets ¾" cabinet grade birch veneer plywood
2 - 6' lengths piano hinge
¼" dowels
3d finishing nails
2" x #8 flathead wood screws
Waterproof wood glue
Wood filler
Door knob and door catch of choice
Polyurethane varnish
Turpentine or paint thinner
Oil base enamel paint in color of choice
Sandpaper, fine/80 grit
Fine steel wool

Tools

Electric circular saw with hollow ground plywood blade
Electric variable speed drill with ¼" auger-type bit
Router with ¾" straight bit and bevel-cutting bit
Nail set
Awl or ice pick
Screwdriver appropriate for screws that come with piano hinges
Hack saw, for cutting piano hinges
Bar clamps
Cutting guides, 4' and 8'

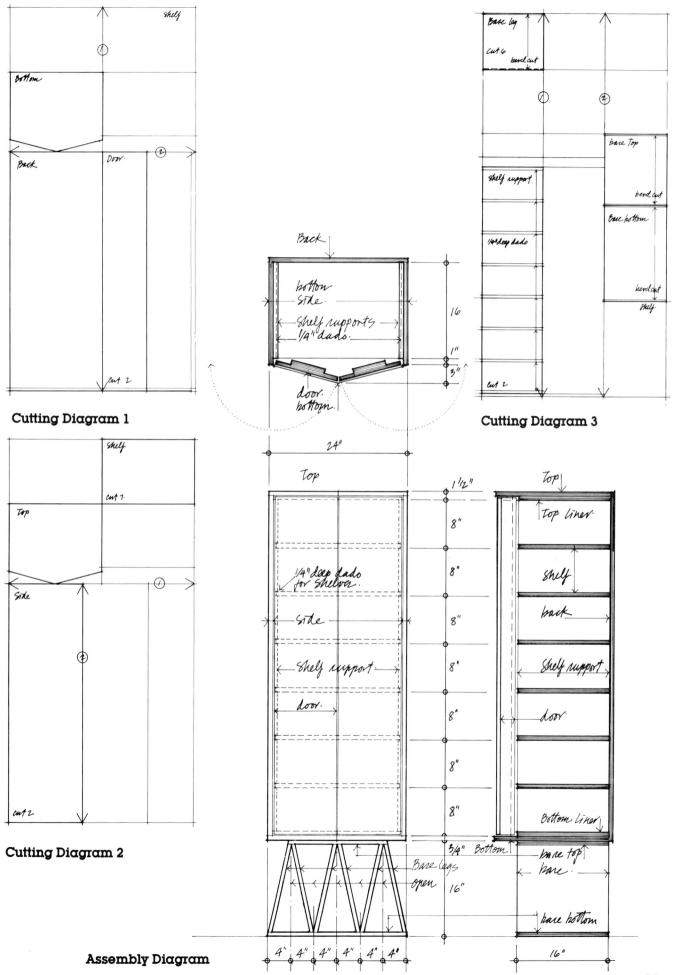

Cutting Diagram 1

Cutting Diagram 2

Cutting Diagram 3

Assembly Diagram

A Versatile Desk for All Ages

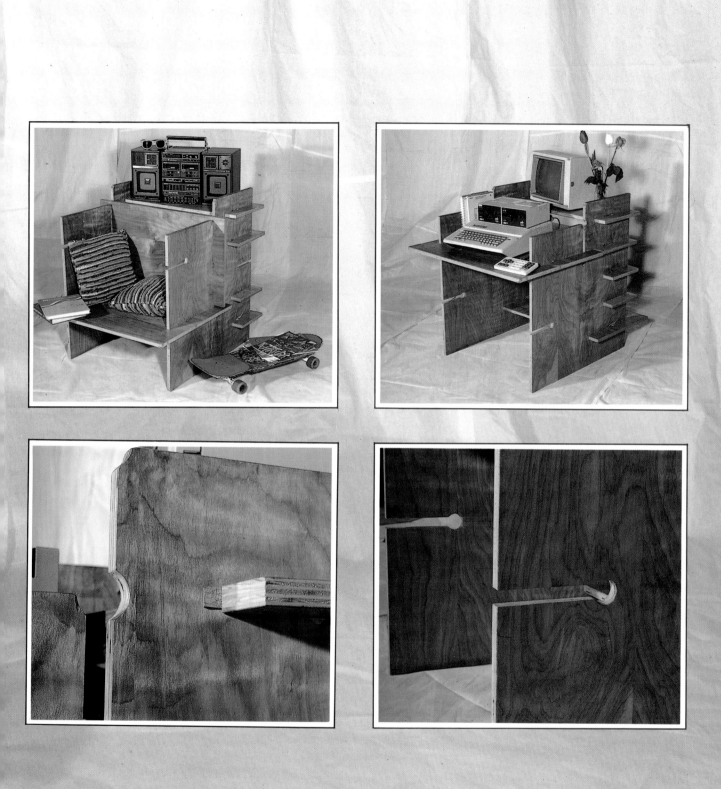

A Versatile Desk for All Ages

Here is a practical solution to your child's changing needs for play area and work station. This versatile desk can be easily assembled in a variety of ways. Today it might be a special home for toys or a private corner for paper and crayons. Tomorrow, just rearrange the shelves for a media center or study nook. Designed with an eye to the future, it's also a special piece of furniture to pass on to younger sister or brother.

INSTRUCTIONS:

Cutting

Measure and mark all straight cuts as shown in Cutting Diagram. Make rough cuts 1 and 2 (indicated by circled numbers) to separate plywood into manageable pieces, with cutting guide clamped in place to assure straight cuts.

Using 1½" bit, drill holes A & B. **NOTE:** When drilling holes, make certain the back side of the plywood is in contact with a flat piece of scrap board. Move the scrap board between drillings for a fresh flat surface. This prevents splintering of the plywood face.

Make cuts 3, 4, and 5, taking care not to extend cuts through the drilled holes. Make Shelf cuts as shown, with cutting guide clamped in place.

When all shelves are cut, stack equal sized shelves on top of each other and trim with the circular saw so they are exactly the same size. **NOTE:** Exact dimensions of shelving will vary because the layout diagram does not include the thickness of the saw blades.

Locate the center of each shelf. Measuring from the center, **not** the sides, locate the center of each slot. Mark the ¾" width of each slot and locate the 1½" diameter holes. Using circle template, trace holes. Mark center of holes for drill bit. Drill holes in shelves.

Measure and mark for slots and holes on one Side. After drilling holes and cutting slots (see below), use Side piece as template for marking holes and slots on other Side piece. This will assure that desk sides are identical.

Refer to Diagram 2 and fabricate jig, using scraps of 1"x4" and 2"x4" lumber. The jig is clamped into place on plywood shelves at each slot to be cut. Space jig's left and right guides so that by making a cut with the saw soleplate resting against the right guide and then with the soleplate resting against the left guide, you will cut a slot the **exact** thickness of the plywood. Slip a scrap of the finished plywood into the slot to test fit; the slots should fit the shelves as snugly as possible and still allow assembly. It is best to determine the spacing between the jig's left and right guides by trial and error, practicing first on available wood scraps. When making slot cuts, check from time to time to assure that the jig has not come out of alignment. Sand all rough edges.

Assembly

It is impossible to make the slots and shelves fit tightly enough to prevent racking, or side-to-side sway. Therefore, it is necessary to fabricate small wedges to be inserted between slot and shelf. Whittle, chisel, or sand wedges from scraps of hardwood (see Diagram 3 for actual size). Insert wedges as shown in detail photo.

This desk can be assembled in a variety of configurations. Study the photos for ideas, and use your own imagination for variations.

Finishing

Using a mixture of 1 part paint thinner to 3 parts polyurethane, finish desk with two or more coats. Allow each coat to dry thoroughly. Lightly sand between coats, and buff lightly with steel wool after final coat.

Materials

1 - 4'x8' sheet ¾" cabinet grade birch veneer plywood
1 quart polyurethane varnish
Turpentine or paint thinner
Scraps of oak or other hardwood, for wedges
Sandpaper, fine/80 grit
Fine steel wool
Miscellaneous scraps of 1"x4" and 2"x4" lumber, for making slot-cutting jig

Tools

Electric circular saw with hollow ground plywood blade
Electric variable speed drill with 1½" auger-type bit
4" and 6" C-clamps
Combination square, for marking slots
Circle template, for marking drill holes
Cutting guide, 6'

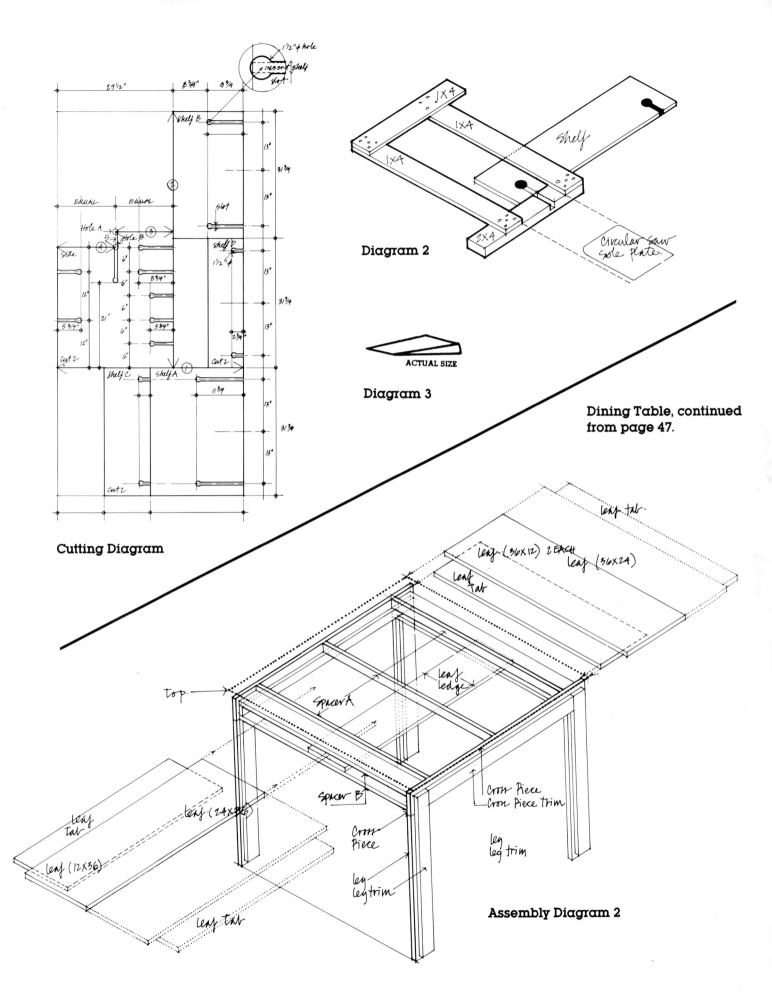

Diagram 2

ACTUAL SIZE

Diagram 3

Dining Table, continued from page 47.

Cutting Diagram

Assembly Diagram 2

A Lightweight Showcase
for Your Collectibles

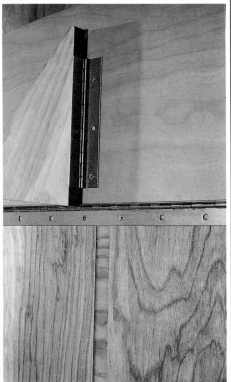

A Lightweight Showcase for Your Collectibles

Bring your favorite knick-knacks out of storage and spotlight them on this tasteful shelf unit. Its free-standing construction makes it a versatile piece of furniture—since it doesn't need a wall for support, it can divide a room's space, cross a corner, or stand out from a wall to create relief and depth. Add a special light fixture for a dramatic effect or use painted accents for a special touch. If you need to store it or move it, just fold it flat in seconds.

INSTRUCTIONS:

Cutting

NOTE: If you rearrange cutting layout to take advantage of the plywood's attractive grain, you may need to buy two sheets of plywood.

Measure and mark all pieces on plywood sheet. Make rough cuts 1 and 2 (indicated by circled numbers) to separate plywood into manageable pieces, with 8' cutting guide clamped in place to assure straight cuts. Mark and cut Shelves, Shelf Brackets, and Back Brace, with 4' cutting guide clamped in place.

The right edges of the Shelves are square cut; the left edges are cut at angles to meet a sloped line on the Back (see Assembly Diagram 1-A). Make angled cuts on left edges of Shelves, with 4' cutting guide clamped in place. **NOTE:** The middle Shelf is wider than other Shelves; project slope in a continuous line outward (see Assembly Diagram 2).

Cut hinges to fit Shelf, Back Brace, and Shelf Bracket dimensions. **NOTE:** Piano hinges come with pre-drilled holes 2 inches apart; cut hinges exactly between holes for ease of handling.

Assembly

Mark shelf locations on Back. Mark center groove for router; using router and ¾" straight bit, make groove no more than 1/16" deep for stabilizing Shelf Brackets in open position. **NOTE:** Make routed groove deeper if it will be painted, so paint doesn't fill up groove.

Using awl or ice pick to start screw holes, attach hinges to back edges of Shelves, and then to Shelf Back (fold shelves up against back for easier access). Fold Shelves down into approximate open position; raise Shelf Brackets in routed groove until they touch Shelf undersides; mark where hinges will go. Attach hinges to top edges of Shelf Brackets. Fold Shelves up and Brackets sideways; attach hinges to undersides of Shelves. Attach hinge to edge of Back Brace; with Back Brace folded down sideways against Back, attach hinge to Back. **NOTE:** This shelf unit's free-standing construction can be unwieldy in a high-traffic area.

Finishing

NOTE: Avoid a drippy mess by finishing pieces without hinges. Apply finish before assembling; or assemble, take apart and finish, reassemble. Apply clear finish before painting edges—if paint is dripped on finished surface, a cloth and mineral spirits will remove it easily.

Using a mixture of 1 part turpentine or paint thinner to 3 parts polyurethane varnish, finish all pieces with three coats. Allow each coat to dry thoroughly. Lightly sand between coats, and buff lightly with steel wool after final coat.

Paint sloped right edge of Back and sloped left edges of Shelves with three coats, sanding lightly between coats. For a special accent, you can also paint the routed groove. Alternatively, shelves can be painted or covered with a laminate surface.

Materials

1 - 4'x8' sheet ¾" cabinet grade birch veneer plywood
2 - 6' lengths piano hinge
1 quart polyurethane varnish
Turpentine or paint thinner
Sandpaper, fine/80 grit
Fine steel wool
Oil base enamel paint, in color of your choice

Tools

Electric circular saw with hollow ground plywood blade
Router with ¾" straight bit, for making groove that fixes shelf brackets in open position
Hack saw, for cutting piano hinges
Awl or ice pick
Screwdriver appropriate for screws that come with piano hinges
Cutting guides, 4' and 8'

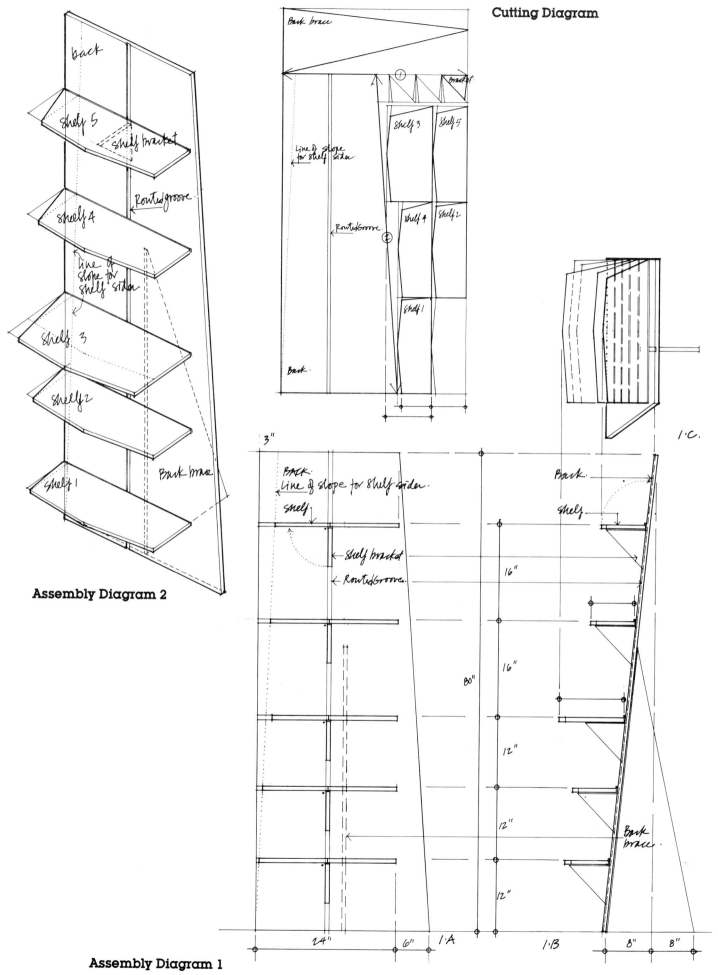

Cutting Diagram

Back brace

bracket

Shelf 3 Shelf 5

Line of slope
for shelf sides

Routed Groove

Shelf 4 Shelf 2

Shelf 1

Back.

back

shelf 5

shelf bracket

Routed groove

shelf 4

line of
slope for
shelf sides

shelf 3

shelf 2

shelf 1

Back brace

Assembly Diagram 2

1·C.

3"

BACK.
Line of slope for shelf sides.

shelf

Back.

shelf

← shelf bracket

← Routed Groove.

16"

80"

16"

12"

12"

Back
brace.

24" 6" 1·A

1·B 8" 8"

12"

Assembly Diagram 1

Knockdown Shelves with Pediment— A Knockout

Knockdown Shelves with Pediment—A Knockout

This architectural pediment-topped shelf unit goes together and knocks down fast, with elevator bolts and wing nuts. And the matte black heads of the elevator bolts add a snazzy design touch to boot. Whether you build it as a bookcase or a wardrobe cabinet with deep shelves, the stately lines of this unit convey updated good taste.

INSTRUCTIONS:

Cutting

Measure and mark all pieces on plywood. Make four rough cuts (indicated by circled numbers) to separate plywood into manageable pieces, with 8' cutting guide clamped in place to assure straight cuts. Cut all other pieces, with 4' cutting guide clamped in place.

Assembly

Locate and mark for drill holes on two Side pieces, following Cutting Diagram 2; drill 5/16" holes through Sides. **NOTE:** Leave pencil marks to help you align drill holes in Side and Back. When drilling holes, make certain the back side of the plywood is in contact with a flat piece of scrap board. Move the scrap board between drillings for a fresh flat surface. This prevents splintering of the plywood face.

Locate, glue, and nail Shelf Supports, Base Supports, and Pediment Supports on insides of Side pieces. Set nails 1/16" below surface. Fill nail holes with wood filler and, when dry, sand until smooth and flush with surface.

Drill 1/4" holes through lengths of dowels or handrails, for the spacers between Sides and wing nuts (see Assembly Diagram 1-C). Using oil base enamel paint in color of your choice, paint spacers with three coats, sanding lightly between coats.

Locate, mark, and drill 1½" holes for spacers in Back, Pediment, and Base. Drill 5/16" holes through edges of Back, Pediment, and Base for the bolts that go into the spacers.

NOTE: Apply polyurethane varnish finish and paint (see below) before assembling. Lay Back flat on floor, on top of a single layer of Shelves to raise Back the thickness of the plywood. Line up Sides along Back (5/16" drilled holes should line up). Insert bolts through Sides, Back, and Spacers; attach washers and wing nuts.

Repeat procedure to attach Base and Pediment. Bolt Fixed Shelf in place, to prevent side-to-side sway. Tighten all wing nuts and raise unit to standing position. Slide Shelves into position between Shelf Supports.

Finishing

Using a mixture of 1 part turpentine or paint thinner to 3 parts polyurethane varnish, finish all pieces with three coats. Allow each coat to dry thoroughly. Lightly sand between coats, and buff lightly with steel wool after final coat. Using oil base enamel paint in color of your choice, paint Shelf Supports with three coats, sanding lightly between coats.

To vary the design, Pediment and/or Shelves can be painted. For a wardrobe cabinet, shelves can be deepened to 24", and a hanging rod and doors can be added; for greater stability, pull recessed Pediment and Base out to front of unit.

Materials

2 - 4'x8' sheets ¾" cabinet grade birch veneer plywood
1½" dowels, or length of handrail, ripped to half-rounds
14 - ¼"x3" elevator bolts (available through specialty nut and bolt companies)
14 wing nuts with washers, to fit elevator bolts
3d finishing nails
Waterproof wood glue
Wood filler
1 quart polyurethane varnish
Turpentine or paint thinner
Sandpaper, fine/80 grit
Fine steel wool
Oil base enamel paint in color of your choice

Tools

Electric circular saw with hollow ground plywood blade
Electric variable speed drill with adjustable auger-type bit
Nail set
C-clamps
Cutting guides, 4' and 8'

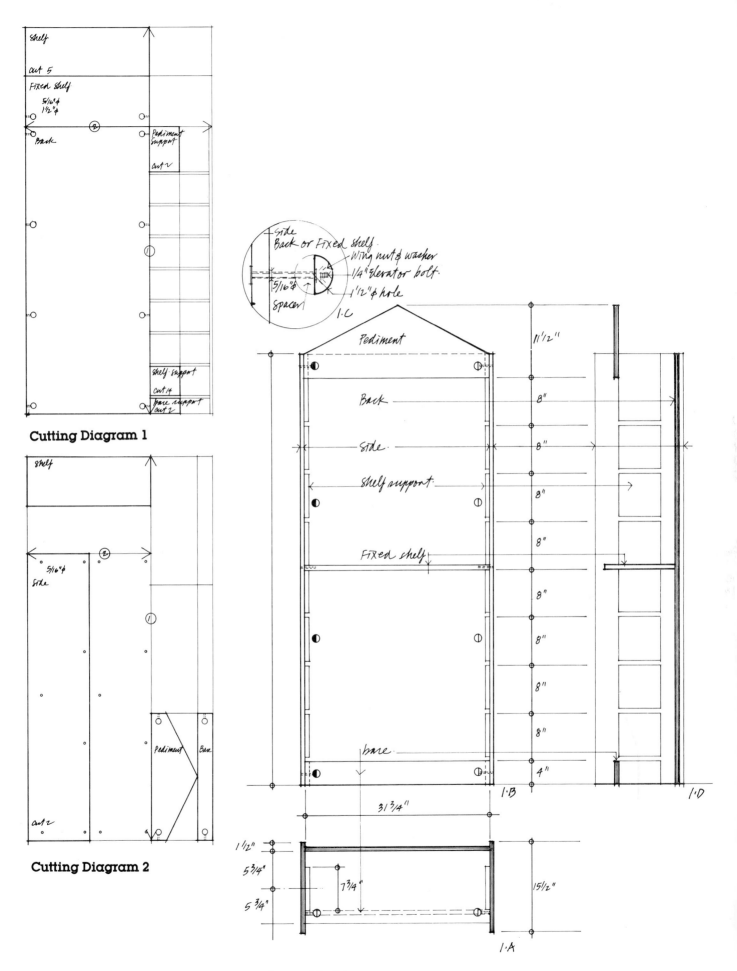

Cutting Diagram 1

Cutting Diagram 2

Assembly Diagram

Sideboard Unit Adds Elegance to Any Room

Sideboard Unit Adds Elegance to Any Room

Contemporary styling combines with classical design to make this sideboard especially versatile. In the dining room, it provides storage space for dinnerware and accessories, as well as a generous surface for serving or setting out buffet offerings. In the living room, it can be a beautiful media center for stereo, VCR, record and tape storage. Add extra shelves inside and the sideboard becomes an elegant shirt cabinet for bedroom or dressing suite. The flexibility of this piece will make it a favored addition to every home.

INSTRUCTIONS:

Cutting

Measure and mark all pieces on plywood. Make four rough cuts (indicated by circled numbers) to separate plywood into manageable pieces, with 8' cutting guide clamped in place to assure straight cuts. **NOTE:** An experienced person can cut all pieces correctly on the first try. However, it is recommended that the Legs be cut and assembled before the Cabinet unit, so that the exact dimensions of the Cabinet can then be determined.

Cut the Legs and Leg Trim, with 4' cutting guide clamped in place. **NOTE:** Cutting Legs will be easier if you use a table saw or radial arm saw. When cutting repetitive pieces the same length, regardless of the type of saw, arrange some kind of stop or block at the end of each cut so that all pieces will be identical lengths.

Cut ¼" dowels into 2½" lengths. Cut ½" dowels into 2" lengths. Cut hinges to fit Door dimensions. **NOTE:** Piano hinges come with pre-drilled holes 2 inches apart; cut hinges exactly between holes for ease of handling.

Assembly

Glue and nail Leg assemblies together; Leg Trim will be applied later. Since the Legs are the same depth as the Cabinet, measure Leg assembly dimensions carefully and then cut the Cabinet components with 4' cutting guide clamped in place. Drill ½" holes through Cabinet sides and Center Divider where shown in Assembly Diagram 1. **NOTE:** When drilling holes, make certain the back side of the plywood is in contact with a flat piece of scrap board. Move the scrap board between drillings for a fresh flat surface. This prevents splintering of the plywood face.

Glue and tap ½" dowel lengths into holes (protruding dowels will support shelves).

Glue and clamp Cabinet together; when glue is dry, drill ¼" holes approximately 2½" deep and 6" apart along glued joints. Apply glue to holes and to ¼" dowel lengths; tap dowels into holes. When glue is dry, sand dowel ends until smooth and flush with surface.

Apply Leg Trim to inside of Legs with glue and nails (these Trim pieces will support the side edges of the Cabinet). To attach Legs to Cabinet, drill and screw through the Legs into the Cabinet sides. To cover screw holes, nail Leg Trim to outside of Legs. Fill holes with wood putty; when completely dry, sand smooth.

Attach hinge to each Door, using awl or ice pick to start screw holes; mount Doors on Cabinet. Attach door catch and door knobs, or drill ½" holes where desired and tap glued ½" dowel lengths into holes for door handles. Slide Shelves into place on dowel supports.

Finishing

The sideboard shown here used a clear finish on all pieces except the front of the Leg Trim. Using a mixture of 1 part turpentine or paint thinner to 3 parts polyurethane varnish, finish sideboard with three coats. Allow each coat to dry thoroughly. Lightly sand between coats, and buff lightly with steel wool after final coat. Using oil base enamel paint in color of your choice, paint Leg Trim with three coats, sanding lightly between coats.

Design variations for finishing include cutting a piece of ¼" glass to fit the sideboard's top, painting the entire piece, painting just the doors, or stenciling the doors for a country look.

Materials

2 - 4'x8' sheets plus scraps ¾" cabinet grade birch veneer plywood
¼" and ½" dowels
2 - 6' lengths piano hinge
1¼" x #6 flathead wood screws
3d finishing nails
Door knobs of choice and door catch
Wood filler
Waterproof wood glue
1 quart polyurethane varnish
Turpentine or paint thinner
Sandpaper, fine/80 grit
Fine steel wool
Oil base enamel paint in color of your choice

Tools

Electric circular saw with hollow ground plywood blade
Electric variable speed drill with ¼" and ½" auger-type bits
Hack saw, for cutting piano hinges
Nail set
Awl or ice pick
Screwdriver appropriate for screws that come with piano hinges
Bar clamps
Cutting guides, 4' and 8'

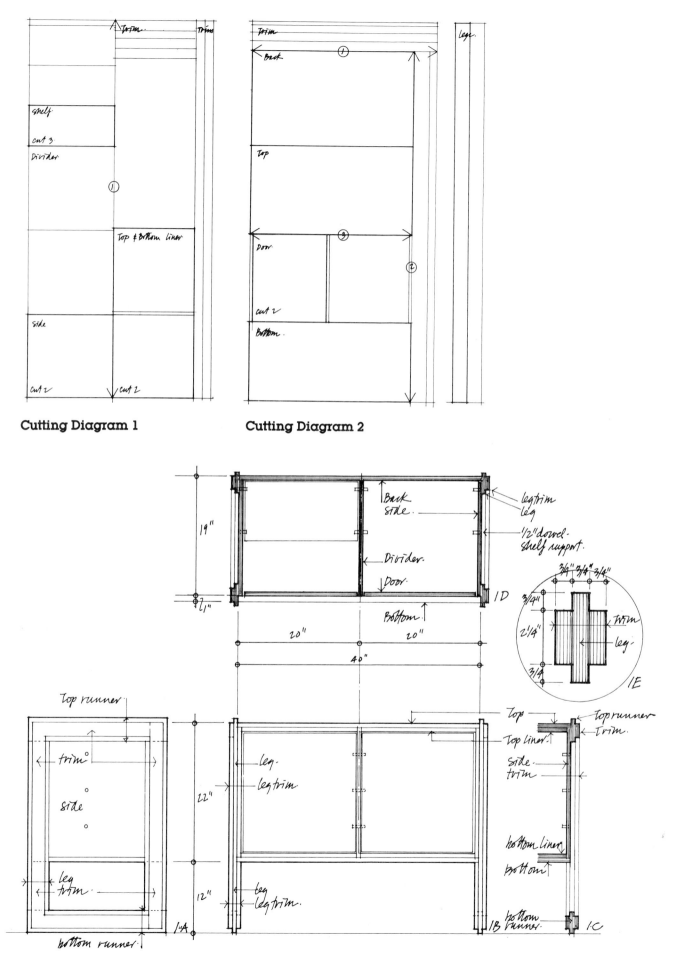

Cutting Diagram 1

Cutting Diagram 2

Assembly Diagram 1

See page 67 for Sideboard Assembly Diagram 2.

Entertain With Style

Entertain With Style

Add a special touch of elegance to all your social affairs with this classy bar. Its storage areas are specially designed to hold tall bottles or decanters, long stem glasses, and other accessories needed for entertaining. Just open the front door—its back side doubles as a water-repellent spot for ice bucket or for slicing limes. Make this piece a truly individual statement with your choices of color, the addition of mirrored surfaces, or a built-in cutting board.

INSTRUCTIONS:

Cutting

NOTE: If you rearrange the cutting layout to take advantage of the plywood's attractive grain, extra plywood may be needed. A table saw and radial arm saw will make ripping and cross-cutting much easier.

Measure and mark all pieces on plywood. Make seven rough cuts (indicated by circled numbers) to separate plywood into manageable pieces, with cutting guide clamped in place to assure straight cuts. **NOTE:** Pieces will be cut to exact dimensions during assembly, to assure correct fit.

Cut dowels into 2½" lengths. Using hack saw, cut piano hinges according to various door dimensions. **NOTE:** Piano hinges come with pre-drilled holes 2 inches apart; cut hinges exactly between holes for ease of handling.

Using router with ¾" straight bit (or size to fit plywood width), make dado grooves 6" apart along the length of a plywood sheet. Cut Shelf Supports to width dimensions shown in Assembly Diagram 1-A.

Assembly

Cut all pieces for Base, with cutting guide clamped in place. Clamp Base together; glue and nail. Set nails 1/16" below surface; fill holes with wood filler. When dry, sand until smooth and flush with surface. Paint Base with three coats of oil base enamel in color of your choice, sanding lightly between coats.

Cut all pieces for two B units, with cutting guide clamped in place. Glue and clamp B units together. Drill ¼" holes approximately 2½" deep and 3" apart along glued joints. Apply glue to holes and dowel lengths; tap dowels into holes. When dry, sand dowel ends until smooth and flush with surface.

Cut all pieces for Unit C to fit dimension; assemble with glue and dowels as above. Cut all pieces for Unit A to fit dimension; assemble with glue and dowels as above.

Glue and screw Unit C to B units (screw heads will be covered by Shelf Supports). Place assembly on Base; screw together from underneath. Position Unit A in place and screw from below.

Glue Top Liners in place in all units (see Assembly Diagram 1-B). Glue Shelf Supports to inside of each compartment. Rip Shelves to half of each width dimension; cut Shelves to exact length dimensions of each compartment. **NOTE:** The arrangement of half-width and full-width shelves is flexible, to accommodate various selections of bottles, glasses, and other items. Unused shelves can be stored in the shelf slot at the base of each unit.

Measure and cut Doors to fit exact dimensions. Cut front Door Facing for Top unit and nail to outside of front Door (Door Facing keeps Door level when in open or horizontal position). Set nails 1/16" below surface and fill with wood filler. When dry, sand until smooth and flush with surface. Paint with three coats of oil base enamel in color of your choice, sanding lightly between coats.

Using awl or ice pick to start screw holes, attach hinge to lower edge of front Door; mount front Door to Unit A. Attach hinges to outside edges of other Doors; mount Doors to other units. Attach door catches.

Finishing

NOTE: For ease of handling, remove all hardware before finishing; re-assemble after finishing.

Using oil base enamel in color of your choice, paint inside of Unit A door with three coats, sanding lightly between coats (this protects surface from

Materials

3-2/3 - 4'x8' sheets plus scraps ¾" cabinet grade birch veneer plywood
2 - 6' lengths piano hinge
¼" dowels
3d finishing nails
1¼" x #6 flathead wood screws
Magnetic touch door catches
Waterproof wood glue
Wood filler
Polyurethane varnish
Turpentine or paint thinner
Oil base enamel in color of choice
Sandpaper, fine/80 grit
Fine steel wool

Tools

Electric circular saw with hollow ground plywood blade
Electric variable speed drill with ¼" auger-type bit
Router with ¾" straight bit, or size to fit plywood width
Hack saw, for cutting piano hinges
Screwdriver appropriate for screws that come with piano hinges
C-clamps and bar clamps
Combination square, for marking
Cutting guides, 4' and 8'

moisture and spills). Finish all unpainted plywood with three coats of a mixture of 3 parts polyurethane varnish and 1 part turpentine or paint thinner. Allow each coat to dry thoroughly. Sand lightly between coats and buff with fine steel wool after the final coat.

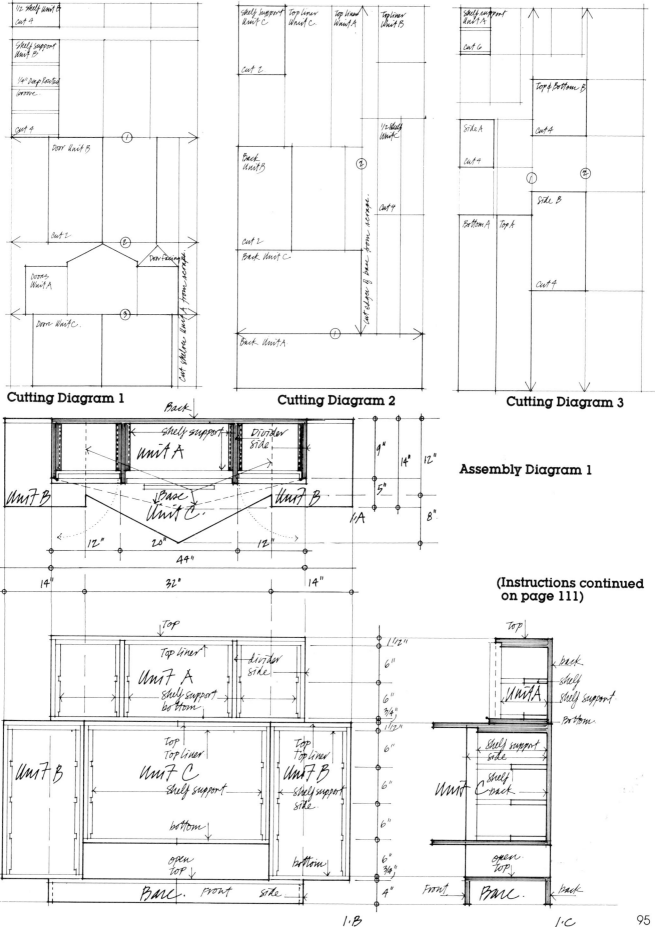

Cutting Diagram 1

Cutting Diagram 2

Cutting Diagram 3

Assembly Diagram 1

(Instructions continued on page 111)

95

Hall Tree Adds Touch of Class

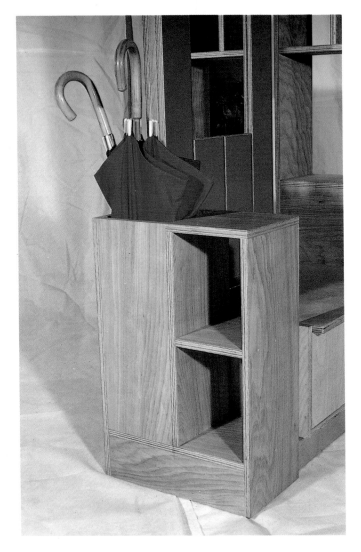

Hall Tree Adds Touch of Class

Before you dash off for another day, here's a beautiful chance to have a last look at yourself and grab your umbrella. When you return, this dignified hall tree is ready for your hat, coat, and other sundries. Open up the hinged seat to store wet galoshes or use the handy shelves to stow away car keys and maps.

INSTRUCTIONS:

Cutting

NOTE: Use of a table saw and radial arm saw will make ripping and cross-cutting much easier.

Measure and mark all pieces on plywood. Make four rough cuts (indicated by circled numbers) to separate plywood into manageable pieces, with cutting guide clamped in place to assure straight cuts.

Mark and cut all pieces of the Arm units, with cutting guide clamped in place (to assure correct fit, other pieces will be cut during assembly). Cut ¼" dowels into 2½" lengths; cut 1½" dowels into 4" lengths.

Assembly

Glue and clamp Arm units together. When glue is dry, drill ¼" holes approximately 2½" deep and 3" apart along glued joints. Apply glue to holes and to 2½" dowel lengths; tap dowels into holes. When dry, sand dowel ends until smooth and flush with surface.

Cut all pieces for Seat unit, with cutting guide clamped in place. Prop Seat Sides upright on working surface. Position Seat Bottom and Seat Front between Sides. Glue and clamp in place; when glue is dry, glue and dowel as above.

Screw Seat Ledge to Seat Side. Glue and dowel Fixed Seat piece to Sides. Using awl or ice pick to start screw holes, attach hinge to rear edge of Hinged Seat; attach Hinged Seat to Fixed Seat piece.

Cut Front Base and Back Base pieces to full arm-to-arm length; screw Front Base and Back Base to each Arm Unit. Place seat unit on Base between Arm units; from inside, screw Seat unit to Base.

Cut Trim pieces and, using router with bevel-cutting bit, bevel edges as shown in Assembly Diagram 1. Using router with ¼" straight bit, make dado groove ¼" deep along edges as shown in Assembly Diagram 1-C (mirror will fit into these grooves).

Glue and nail Trim to Back. Set nails 1/16" below surface and fill with wood filler; when dry, sand until smooth and flush with surface. Paint Trim with three coats of oil base enamel in color of your choice, sanding lightly between coats.

Cut Back to exact dimensions of assembled unit. Position Back so that lower edge of Trim rests on Fixed Seat piece; bolt Back in place. Cut Pediment to exact dimension; finish with three coats (see below).

Drill 1½" holes for dowel pegs, where desired. Finish pegs with three coats (see below). Apply glue to pegs and tap into holes.

Slide mirror into grooved recess. Position Pediment in place above mirror; screw Pediment to Back from behind (this Pediment can be removed if the mirror must be replaced).

Finishing

NOTE: For ease of finishing, remove Back, Seat unit, and Base from Arm units. Finish each component separately and then reassemble.

Using a mixture of 3 parts polyurethane varnish to 1 part turpentine or paint thinner, finish unpainted plywood with 3 coats. Allow each coat to dry thoroughly. Sand lightly between coats and buff with fine steel wool after the final coat.

Materials

2 - 4'x8' sheets (or 1 sheet plus scraps) ¾" cabinet grade birch veneer
¼" mirror to fit dimensions
1 - 2' length piano hinge
¼" and 1½" dowels
3d finishing nails
4 - ¼" x2" elevator or carriage bolts
Waterproof wood glue
Polyurethane varnish
Turpentine or paint thinner
Sandpaper, fine/80 grit
Fine steel wool

Tools

Electric circular saw with hollow ground plywood blade
Electric variable speed drill with ¼" and 1½" auger-type bits
Router with ¼" straight bit and bevel-cutting bit
Nail set
Awl or ice pick
Screwdriver appropriate for screws that come with piano hinge
Cutting guides, 4' and 8'

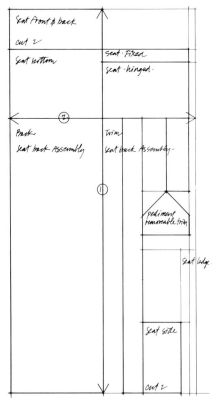

Cutting Diagram 1

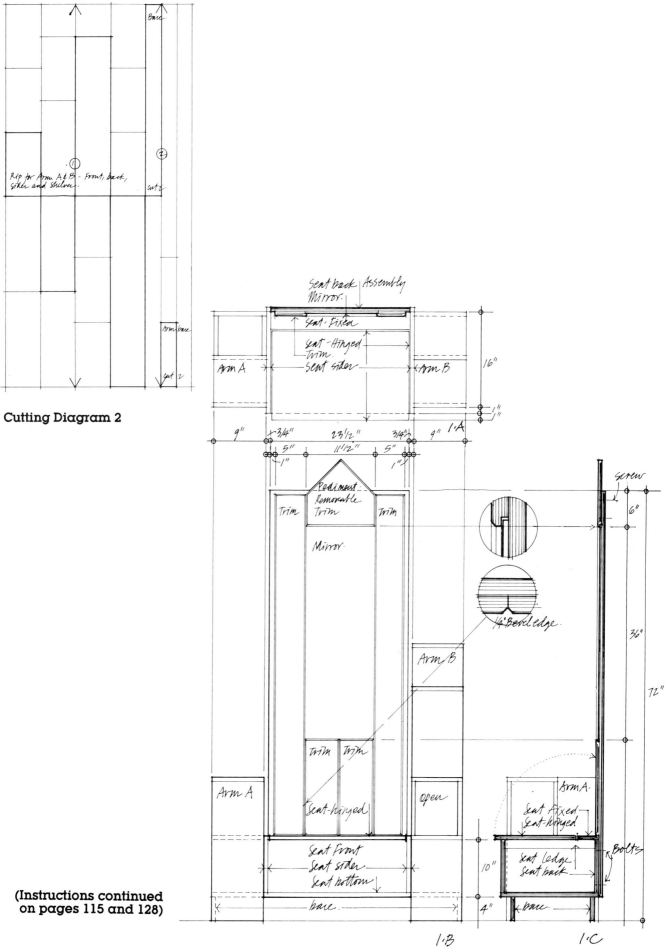

Cutting Diagram 2

Rip for Arm A & B - Front, back, sides and shelves.

Base

Arm base

cut 2

Seat back / Assembly

Mirror

Seat - Fixed

Seat - Hinged

Trim

Seat sides

Arm A

Arm B

16"

1"

1"

9"

3/4"

23 1/2"

3/4"

9"

1.A

5"

11 1/2"

5"

1"

1"

Pediment-
Removable

Trim

Trim

Trim

Mirror

screw

6"

1/4" Bead Edge

36"

72"

Arm B

Trim

Trim

Arm A

Open

Seat-hinged

Arm A

Seat fixed
Seat-hinged

Seat front

Seat sides

Seat bottom

Seat Ledge
Seat back

10"

Bolts

base

base

4"

1.B

1.C

(Instructions continued on pages 115 and 128)

Assembly Diagram 1

4. Extravagances...

A Child's Dream House

A Child's Dream House

Create this exciting playhouse for your children, and to them it will be magical kingdom, fortress, private clubhouse, and desert tent all rolled into one. Its modular construction allows various arrangements as well as easy disassembly for storage or moving. Use canvas or muslin for an easily installed roof or, for a touch of energized color, drape with striped beach towels.

INSTRUCTIONS:

Cutting and Assembly

NOTE: For flexibility in arrangements of playhouse, extra columns and wall panels are included in cutting layout. If playhouse is to be a permanent and unchanging structure, fewer columns and wall panels may be needed.

Measure and mark all pieces on plywood, following Cutting Diagrams. Make six rough cuts (indicated by circled numbers) to separate plywood into manageable pieces. Cut all pieces for the various sizes of Cross (+) Columns and Flat Columns. **NOTE:** When cutting repetitive pieces the same length, arrange some kind of stop or block at the end of each cut so that all pieces will be identical lengths. Cut various sizes of Tabs and Spacers.

Assemble all Cross Columns and Flat Columns with glue and nails, following Assembly Diagram 1. Attach Tabs to all Cross Columns and Flat Columns with glue and nails, where shown in Assembly Diagram 3.

Draw a 4' square on working surface and position Cross Columns and Flat Columns upright on drawing (see Assembly Diagram 1). Measure dimensions between columns and cut Wall Panels to fit these dimensions. Glue and nail Tabs to back sides of Wall Panels where shown in Assembly Diagram 2.

Measure and cut Pediments. Glue and nail Trim to front and back of Pediments, where shown in Assembly Diagram 3. Using 1⅝" auger-type bit, drill holes ¾" deep in Tabs as shown (dowels that hold fabric roof fit in these holes).

Finishing

If desired, set all nails 1/16" below surface and fill nail holes with wood filler. When dry, sand until smooth and flush with surface.

Using a mixture of 1 part turpentine or paint thinner and 3 parts polyurethane varnish, finish all pieces with 2 coats, sanding lightly between coats.

Using oil base enamel in color(s) of your choice, apply 3 coats as you desire, sanding lightly between coats. In the playhouse shown here, paint was applied to the back sides of Tabs, faces of Flat Columns, Pediment Tabs, and the inside corners of the Cross Columns. Finish remaining unpainted surfaces with one more coat of polyurethane varnish and buff lightly with fine steel wool.

Assemble the playhouse by interlocking the pieces (there is no need for nails or fasteners). **NOTE:** If playhouse will be a permanent and unchanging structure, it may be screwed together for greater stability.

Measure and cut dowels to fit between Pediments. Cut fabric of choice (or use beach towels) to fit over Pediments; make casing to hold dowels, or lash fabric to dowels using grommets and cord, or wrap fabric over dowels and safety pin in place, or use buttons and buttonholes to hold fabric in place.

Materials

2 - 4'x8' sheets, or scraps, ¾" cabinet grade birch veneer plywood
1⅝" dowels
Canvas, beach towels, or fabric of choice
3d finishing nails
Waterproof wood glue
Polyurethane varnish
Turpentine or paint thinner
Sandpaper, fine/80 grit
Fine steel wool
Oil base enamel in color of choice

Tools

Electric circular saw with hollow ground plywood blade
Table saw, for ripping lengths
Radial arm saw, for cross-cutting
Electric variable speed drill with 1⅝" auger-type bit, or size to fit dowels

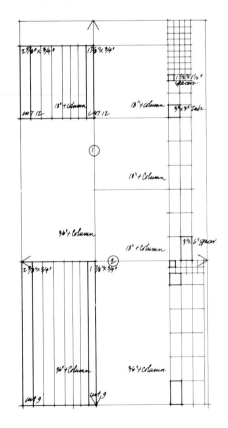

Cutting Diagram 1

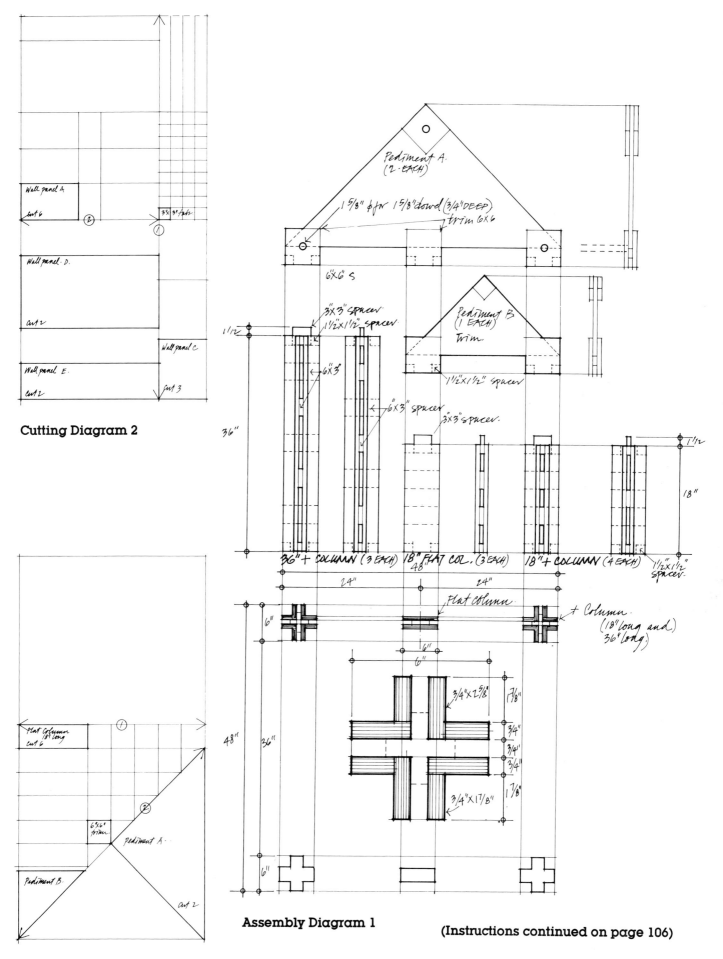

Cutting Diagram 2

Wall panel A
cut 6 ②

38 3" tabs ①

Wall panel D.
cut 2

Wall panel C
cut 3

Wall panel E.
cut 2

Cutting Diagram 3

Flat Column
18" long
cut 6 ①

6"x6"
trim

Pediment A.

Pediment B.

cut 2 ②

Pediment A.
(2 EACH)

1 5/8" ∅ for 1 5/8" dowel (3/4" DEEP)
trim 6x6

6"x6" S

3"x3" spacer.
1 1/2"x1 1/2" spacer

6"x3"

Pediment B
(1 EACH)
Trim.

1 1/2"x1 1/2" spacer

6"x3" spacer

3"x3" spacer.

36"

18"

36"+ COLUMN (3 EACH)   18" FLAT COL. (3 EACH)   18"+ COLUMN (4 EACH)
48   1 1/2"x1 1/2"
                                                    spacer.

24"   24"

Flat column
+ Column.
(18" long and)
36" long)

6"
6"
6"

48"   36"

3/4"x2 5/8"   7/8"
3/4"
3/4"
3/4"
3/4"x1 7/8"   1 7/8"

6"

Assembly Diagram 1

(Instructions continued on page 106)

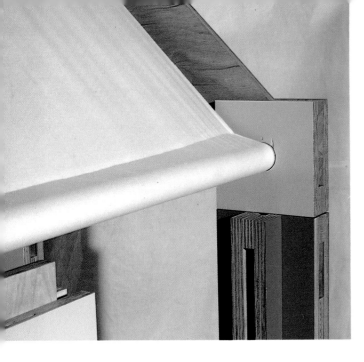

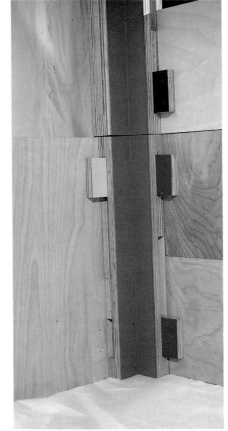

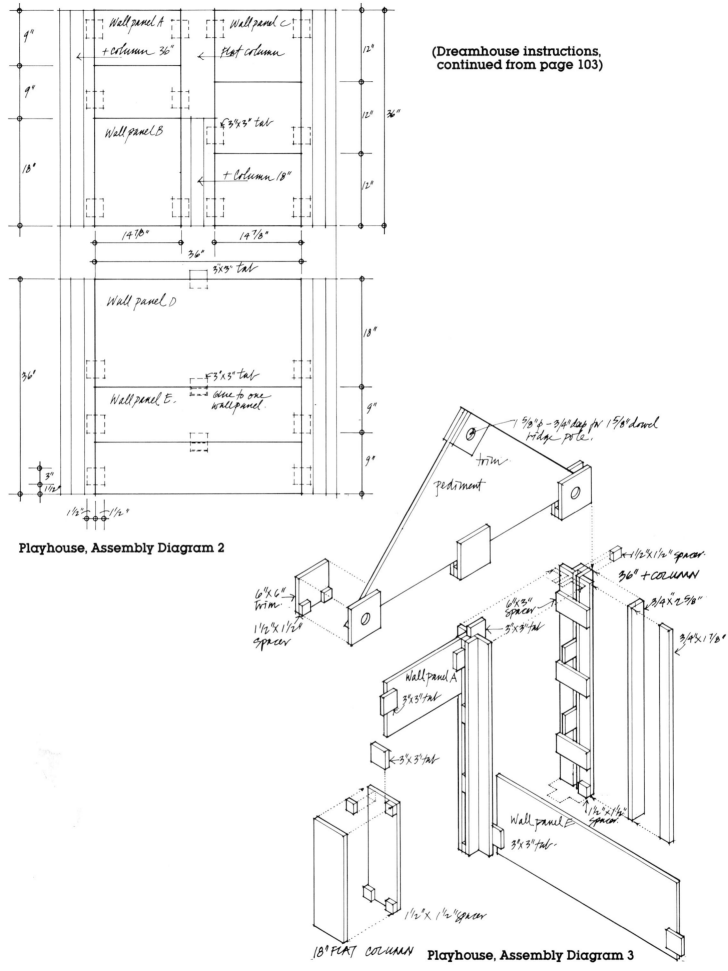

9"

9"

18"

Wall panel A

+ column 36"

Wall panel B

Wall panel C

Flat column

←3"x3" tab

+ Column 18"

12"

12" 36"

12"

14⅞"   14⅞"

36"

3"x3" tab

Wall panel D

Wall panel E.

←3"x3" tab

←3"x3" tab

Glue to one
wall panel.

18"

9"

9"

36'

3"

1½"

1½"   1½"

Playhouse, Assembly Diagram 2

1 ⅝"ø - 3/4" deep for 1⅝" dowel
ridge pole.

trim

pediment

6"x6"
Trim.

1½"x1½"
spacer

1½"x1½" spacer.

36" + COLUMN

6"x3"
spacer

3"x3" tab

3/4"x2⅝"

3/4"x1⅞"

Wall panel A

3"x3" tab

←3"x3" tab

1½"x1½"
spacer

Wall panel E

3"x3" tab.

1½"x 1½" spacer

18" FLAT COLUMN

Playhouse, Assembly Diagram 3

Wall-Mounted Rack Provides Convenient Storage

Spice jars and condiment bottles seem to multiply by themselves, as do first aid preparations and beauty notions, and yet kitchen and bathroom storage is usually at a premium. This wall-mounted unit gives just the kind of space you need and yet doesn't claim valuable counter space. Dressed up with paint, fancy knobs, or mirrors, it will fit right in wherever you put it.

Materials

1/3 sheet, or scraps, 3/4" cabinet grade birch veneer plywood
3d finishing nails
Wood filler
Waterproof wood glue
Door knobs and door catch of choice
Pivot-type cabinet hinges, or 4' length piano hinge
Polyurethane varnish
Turpentine or paint thinner
Sandpaper, fine/80 grit
Fine steel wool
Oil base enamel in color of choice

Tools

Table saw, for ripping lengths
Radial arm saw, for cross cutting
Hack saw, for cutting piano hinge
Router with ¾" straight bit, or size to fit plywood width
Bar clamps
Nail set
Awl or ice pick
Screwdriver appropriate for screws that come with piano hinges

INSTRUCTIONS:
Cutting

NOTE: If cabinet is built as a spice rack, dimensions may be adjusted to accommodate most common heights of bottles and jars.

Measure, mark, and cut all pieces except Doors. Cut piano hinge to fit Door dimensions. **NOTE:** Piano hinges come with pre-drilled holes 2 inches apart; cut hinges exactly between holes for ease of handling.

Assembly

Clamp Sides, Divider, Top, and Bottom together to make cabinet frame. Glue and nail; set nails 1/16" below surface and fill with wood filler. When dry, sand until smooth and flush with surface.

With router and ¾" straight bit, make dado grooves in Shelf Supports where shown. Glue Shelf Supports to inside of Cabinet compartments. When dry, slide Shelves into place.

Cut Doors to exact dimensions of cabinet frame. Using awl or ice pick to start screw holes, attach piano hinges or cabinet hinges to outside edges of Doors; mount Doors to frame. Attach door knobs and door catch.

Finishing

NOTE: For ease of handling, take Doors and hardware off before finishing.

Paint outside of cabinet frame with three coats of oil base enamel in color of your choice, sanding lightly between coats.

Using a mixture of 1 part turpentine or paint thinner to 3 parts polyurethane varnish, finish Doors, Shelves, and insides with three coats. Allow each coat to dry thoroughly. Sand lightly between coats and buff lightly with steel wool after final coat.

Cabinet may be screwed directly to the wall. Alternatively, a frame may be attached to the wall and the cabinet screwed to the frame. The cabinet may also be set on a counter.

If cabinet will be used in the bathroom, vary the design by adding mirrors to the door. A light fixture may also be incorporated into the bottom of the unit.

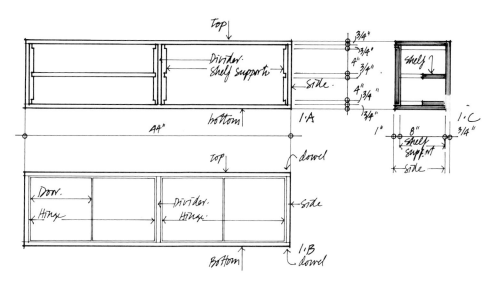

Assembly Diagram

Build Your Own Masterpiece

Build Your Own Masterpiece

Here is a great way to use up plywood scraps of various sizes, with the added attraction of ending up with a very unique set of building blocks. You can let the architect in you come out while you build your own post-modern monuments or use your mathematical prowess to arrange an impossible maze. Whatever direction you take, these blocks will keep you occupied for hours on end as you continue to pursue "just one more option." When you tire of model-building, have fun with the other feature of these blocks—find the puzzles created by the plywood grain and the painted patterns.

INSTRUCTIONS:

Cutting

NOTE: The finished stack of building blocks is a 12" cube if plywood is a full ¾" width. Each of the 12"x12" Cutting Patterns is also a puzzle by virtue of the wood grain in the plywood and the applied Color Patterns.

Finish plywood pieces before cutting (see below). Rough cut plywood sheet into approximate 13" widths. Cut 13" widths into 13"x13" squares to aid in selecting the wood grain for the patterns.

Set a jig on the table of the radial arm saw which will make an accurate 6" cut. Sample cut 2 scraps and lay them side by side to verify that the pieces make an accurate 12" width.

Cut loose block A which, when placed firmly against the jig, will make an accurate 3" cut (see Diagram 1). Sample cut 4 scraps and lay side by side to verify that the 4 equal pieces make an accurate 12" width.

Cut loose block B which, when placed firmly against the jig and loose block A, will make an accurate 1½" cut. Sample cut 8 scraps and lay side by side to verify that the 8 equal pieces make an accurate 12" width.

Cut loose block C which, when placed firmly against the jig and loose blocks A and B, will make an accurate ¾" cut. Sample cut 8 scraps and lay side by side to verify that the 8 equal pieces will make an accurate 6" width.

Make all cuts, following Cutting Patterns 1-A, 1-B, 1-C, 1-D, 1-E, and 1-F; sand all edges of plywood. Assemble Cutting Patterns and make Color Patterns 2-A, 2-B, 2-C, 2-D, 2-E, and 2-F.

Finishing

Using a mixture of 1 part turpentine or paint thinner to 3 parts polyurethane varnish, finish plywood with 3 coats, before cutting. Sand lightly between coats and buff lightly with fine steel wool after the final coat. Mask Color Patterns with tape or cardboard; paint Color Patterns with 3 coats of oil base enamel in color of your choice, sanding lightly between coats.

Materials

¾ sheet, or scraps, ¾" cabinet grade birch veneer plywood
Polyurethane varnish
Turpentine or paint thinner
Oil base enamel in color of choice
Masking tape or cardboard, for masking color patterns
Sandpaper, fine/80 grit
Fine steel wool

Tools

Radial arm saw with hollow ground plywood blade

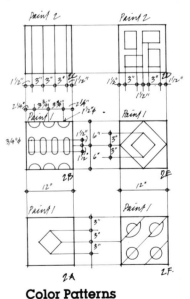

Color Patterns

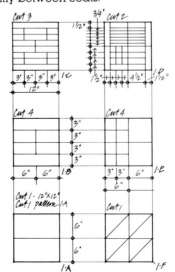

Cutting Patterns

Diagram 1

110

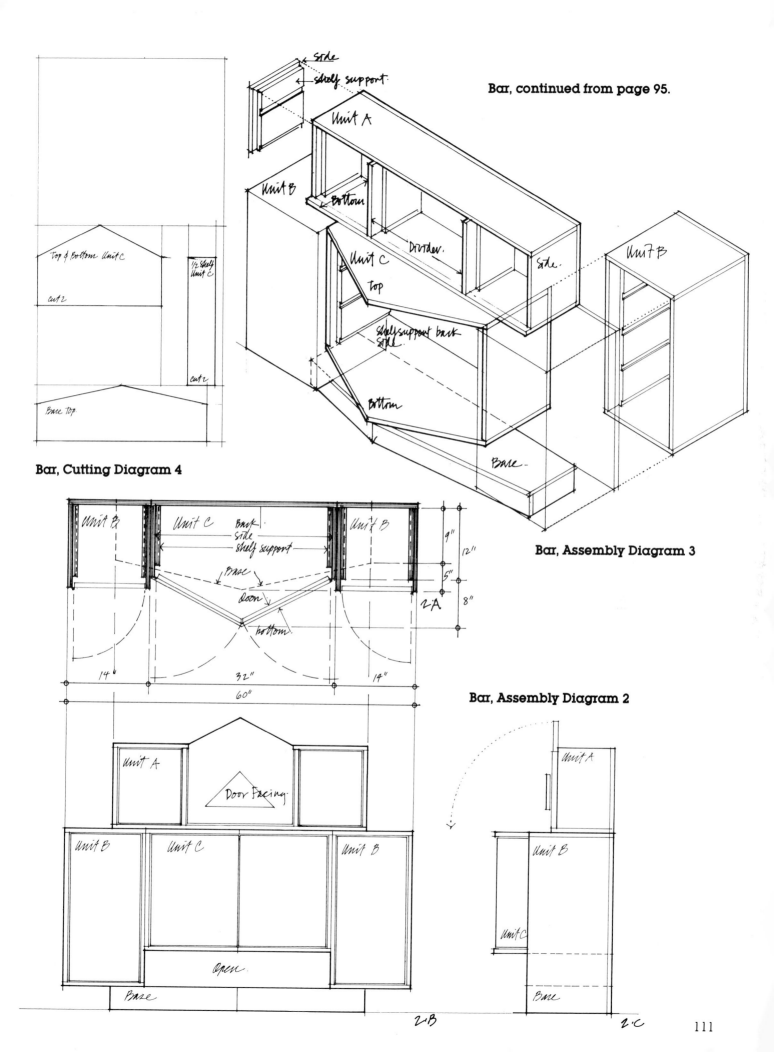

side

shelf support

Bar, continued from page 95.

Unit A

Unit B

Bottom

Divider.

Unit C

Top

Side.

Unit B

shelf support back
side

Bottom

Base.

Top & Bottom Unit C

cut 2

½ shelf
Unit C

Base Top.

cut 2

Bar, Cutting Diagram 4

Unit B

Unit C

Back.
side
shelf support

Unit B

Base

Door

Bottom

9"

12"

5"

2·A

8"

Bar, Assembly Diagram 3

14"

32"

14"

60"

Bar, Assembly Diagram 2

Unit A

Door Facing.

Unit A

Unit B

Unit C

Unit B

Unit B

Unit C

Open.

Base

Base

2·B

2·C

Stacking Trays for a Change of Pace

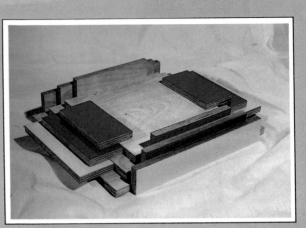

Serve Up Some Style from Scraps

Stacking Trays for a Change of Pace

You know how handy trays can be—for buffet parties, lazy meals on the floor in front of the fireplace, or for a champagne breakfast in bed on a weekend morning. It's even handier to have lots of trays, but storing them often becomes a problem. These colorful stacking trays are a perfect solution. They don't take up much storage space and the three different sizes give you the variety you need for breakfast, lunch, dinner, or snack.

INSTRUCTIONS:

Cutting

NOTE: Because Handles and Sidebars are such small pieces, use of a table saw will give greater control when cutting.

Measure and mark all pieces, following Diagram 1. Cut all pieces, with cutting guide clamped in place to assure straight cuts.

Assembly

Glue and nail Handles and Sidebars to Tray Bases. Set nails 1/16" below surface. Fill nail holes with wood filler; when filler is dry, sand smooth.

Finishing

Using a mixture of 1 part turpentine or paint thinner to 3 parts polyurethane varnish, finish trays with three coats. Allow each coat to dry thoroughly. Lightly sand between coats, and buff lightly with steel wool after final coat. Using oil base enamel in colors of your choice, paint Handles and Sidebars with three coats, sanding lightly between coats.

Materials

Plywood scraps from other projects in this book
3d finishing nails
Wood filler
Waterproof wood glue
Polyurethane varnish
Turpentine or paint thinner
Sandpaper, fine/80 grit
Fine steel wool
Oil base enamel paint, in color(s) of your choice

Tools

Electric circular saw with hollow ground plywood blade
Nail set
Cutting guide, 4'

Serve Up Some Style from Scraps

You can carry edible goodies for a cozy hearthside snack on this tray and not worry about things sliding—the dowel handles assure a good grip. The slat construction gives the tray an airy look and its open handles make for instant storage—just hang it up on end. This is a perfect project for using up plywood scraps!

INSTRUCTIONS:

Cutting

NOTE: While hand-held saws can be used for all cuts, a table saw and radial arm saw will vastly facilitate cutting, and a drill press will make repetitive hole-drilling much easier.

Measure and cut all pieces, following Diagram 1. **NOTE:** When cutting repetitive pieces the same length, arrange some kind of stop or block at the end of each cut so that all pieces will be identical lengths.

Assembly

Drill ¼" holes in slats. **NOTE:** When drilling holes, make certain the back side of the plywood is in contact with a flat piece of scrap board. Move the scrap board between drillings for a fresh flat surface. This prevents splintering of the plywood face. Cut ¼" dowels to width of tray. Glue ends of dowels and insert. Clamp until glue is dry. Drill ½" holes in handles. Cut ½" dowels to fit handles and insert.

Finishing

Using a mixture of 1 part turpentine or paint thinner to 3 parts polyurethane

Materials

Assorted plywood scraps from other projects in this book
¼" and ½" dowels
Waterproof wood glue
Polyurethane varnish
Turpentine or paint thinner
Sandpaper, fine/80 grit
Fine steel wool
Oil base enamel paint in color of your choice

Tools

Table saw, for ripping slats
Radial arm saw, for cutting lengths
Electric variable speed drill, or drill press, with ¼" and ½" auger-type bits
Bar clamps

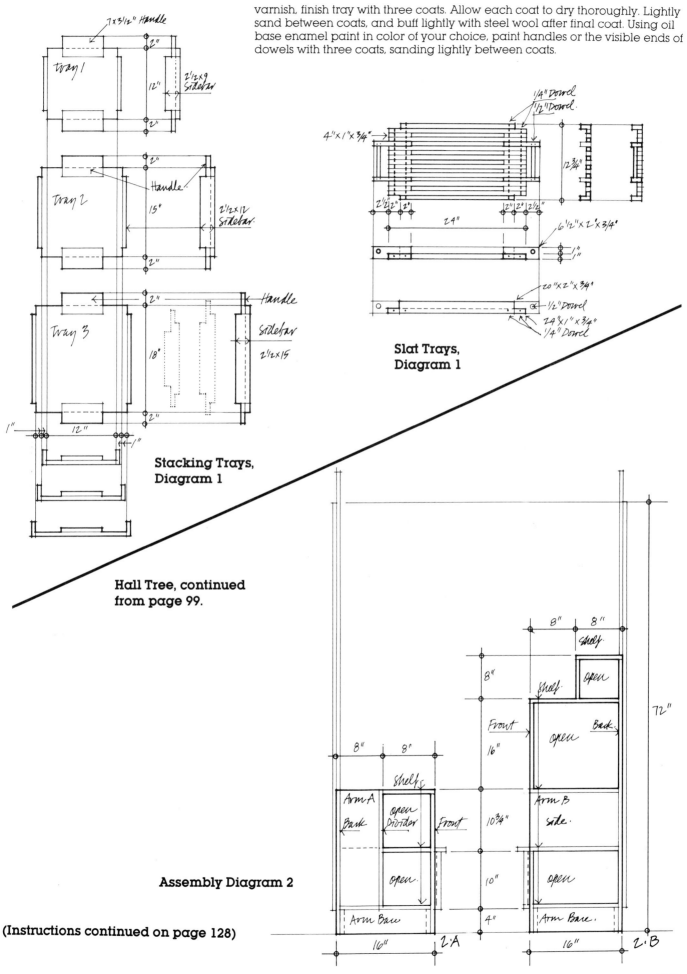

varnish, finish tray with three coats. Allow each coat to dry thoroughly. Lightly sand between coats, and buff lightly with steel wool after final coat. Using oil base enamel paint in color of your choice, paint handles or the visible ends of dowels with three coats, sanding lightly between coats.

Slat Trays, Diagram 1

Stacking Trays, Diagram 1

Hall Tree, continued from page 99.

Assembly Diagram 2

(Instructions continued on page 128)

Floor Lamp Adds a Soft Touch

Marking Time Beautifully

The classical stature of a grandfather clock makes it an important family heirloom as well as a time-keeper. Here, the clock design is modernized to create a whole new style of keepsake. The simple lines complement contemporary clock faces and the recessed cabinet adds dimension as well as a place for small treasures. The removable clock face makes the task of setting time a simple one.

INSTRUCTIONS:

Cutting

NOTE: Use of a table saw or radial arm saw will make cutting small pieces much easier.

Measure and mark all pieces, following Cutting Diagram. Cut all pieces, with cutting guides clamped in place to assure straight cuts. **NOTE:** To assure continuous vertical grain, cut entire Front to width; Front piece will be cut apart after Sides and Shelves are assembled.

Cut dowels into 2½" lengths. Cut hinge to fit Door dimension. **NOTE:** Piano hinges come with pre-drilled holes 2 inches apart; cut hinges exactly between holes for ease of handling.

Assembly

Glue and clamp Sides to Back. Drill ¼" holes approximately 2½" deep and 3" apart along glued joints. Apply glue to holes and dowel lengths; tap dowels into holes. When glue is dry, sand dowels until smooth and flush with surface.

Glue and clamp Shelves in place; glue and dowel as above.

Measure from bottom of clock up to first shelf; cut this dimension off Front, for Bottom Facing. Measure and cut Door to correct length. Measure and cut Top Facing to correct length. Glue and clamp Top Facing and Bottom Facing in place; glue and dowel as above.

Rip small amount off of each side of Door, to accommodate hinge and opening allowance. Using awl or ice pick to start screw holes, attach hinge to door and then mount door on clock. Attach door pull and door catch. Install electrical connections and clock works appropriate to type chosen.

Finishing

Using a mixture of 1 part turpentine or paint thinner to 3 parts polyurethane varnish, finish clock with three coats. Allow each coat to dry thoroughly. Lightly sand between coats, and buff lightly with steel wool after final coat. Set clock to your local time zone or time zone of choice.

Materials

½ sheet, or scraps, ¾" cabinet grade birch veneer plywood
¼" dowels
1 - 3' length piano hinge
Waterproof wood glue
Door pull and door catch of choice
Electric or quartz clock works
Lamp cord for electric clock
Polyurethane varnish
Turpentine or paint thinner

Tools

Electric circular saw with hollow ground plywood blade
Electric variable speed drill with ¼" auger-type bit
Bar clamps
Awl or ice pick
Screwdriver appropriate to screws that come with piano hinges
Cutting guides, 4' and 8'
Hole-cutting saw for installation of clock, depending on type chosen

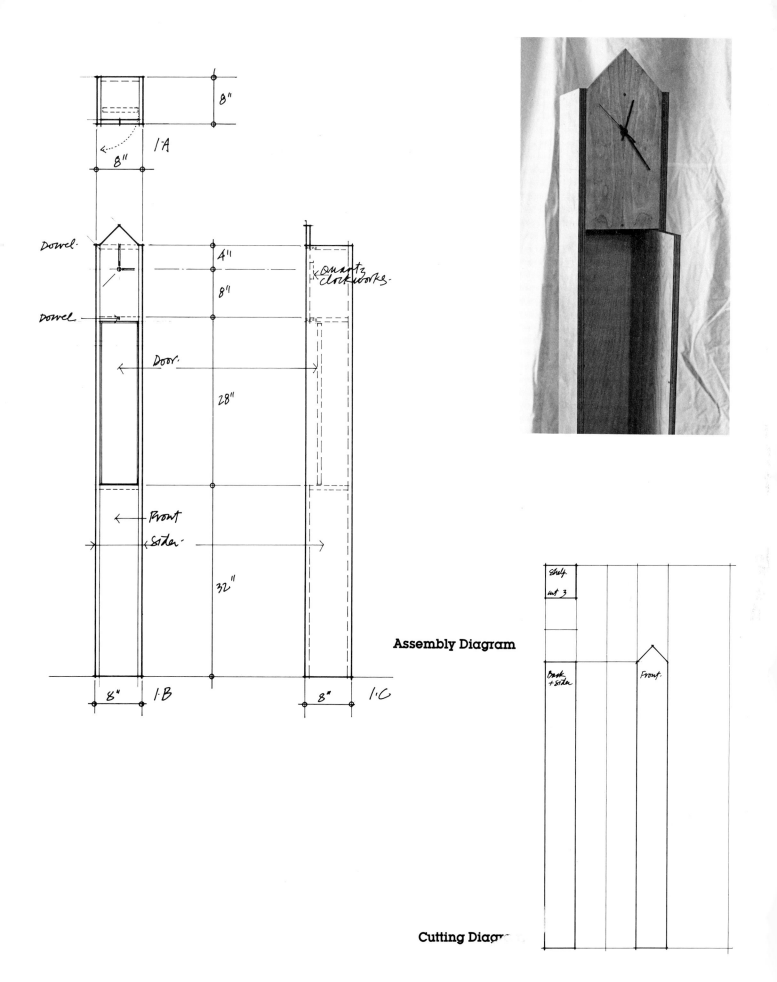

8"

1·A

8"

Dowel

Dowel

Door.

Front

Sides.

4"

8"

28"

32"

Quartz
Clockworks.

1·B

8"

8"

1·C

Assembly Diagram

Shelf.
cut 3

Back
+ sides

Front.

Cutting Diagram

Deco Lamp Glows Softly

Keep Table Linens Beautifully Close at Hand

Deco Lamp Glows Softly

For the ultimate in atmosphere, make this lamp out of plywood scraps. Its layers of tinted plastic allow light to radiate like soft sunlight, gently illuminating dark corners and softening the hard edges created by bright lights. The unusual design of this lamp transforms it from an ordinary light source into sculpture!

INSTRUCTIONS:

Cutting and Assembly

Cut pieces for Light Box, following dimensions in Diagram 1. Glue and nail Light Box together; set nails 1/16" below surface and fill nail holes with wood filler. When dry, sand until smooth and flush with surface.

Using drill with 1/2" auger-type bit, drill Light Holes every 3" where shown in Diagram 1. **NOTE:** When drilling holes, make certain the back side of the plywood is in contact with a flat piece of scrap board. Move the scrap board between drillings for a fresh flat surface. This prevents splintering of the plywood face.

Nail Legs to bottom of Light Box. Using router with 3/4" bit, make groove 1/16" deep on side, as shown in Diagram 2.

Glue and nail layers of Light Base together. Fill nail holes on any exposed surface with wood filler. When dry, sand until smooth and flush with surface.

Cut pieces of plywood and thermoplastic for Laminated Inset. **NOTE:** When cutting repetitive pieces the same length, arrange some kind of stop or block at the end of each cut so that all pieces will be identical lengths.

Glue alternating layers of plywood and thermoplastic together with contact cement. Clamp together and when dry, sand all outside edges with belt sander until smooth.

Install lamp sockets inside Light Box. Install wiring, in-line on-off switch, and plug.

Finishing

Using oil base enamel in color(s) of your choice, paint outside of Light Box, Base, routed groove, and other desired surfaces with three coats, sanding lightly between coats.

Using a mixture of 1 part turpentine or paint thinner and 3 parts polyurethane varnish, finish all edges of plywood and thermoplastic with 3 coats, sanding lightly between coats and buffing with fine steel wool after the final coat.

Slide Light Box onto Base and position Laminated Inset in Light Box.

Materials

Plywood scraps
Tinted Acrilite GP or Plexiglas thermoplastic
3d finishing nails
Waterproof wood glue
Wood filler
Contact cement
2 lamp sockets
Lamp cord
In-line on-off switch
Plug
Polyurethane varnish
Turpentine or paint thinner
Sandpaper, fine/80 grit
Fine steel wool
Oil base enamel in color of choice
2 - 25-watt light bulbs

Tools

Table saw, for ripping lengths
Radial arm saw, for cross-cutting
Electric variable speed drill with 1/2" auger-type bit
Router with 3/4" straight bit
Nail set
Belt sander
Bar clamps

Keep Table Linens Beautifully Close at Hand

This special storage cabinet was designed to adapt to your needs—bin sizes can be easily changed to accommodate your tablecloths, placemats, and napkins, no matter how you fold them. The slatted bottom keeps air flowing so linens stay fresh and dry. This li... cabinet is attractive enough to keep your linens out a'' ... ne, and close at hand when you need them.

INSTRUCTIONS:

Cutting

NOTE: Sides, Front, and Back dimensions can be adjusted to make the cabinet deeper, to hold more linens. The napkin side size can be adjusted to match the way you fold your napkins.

Measure and mark all pieces, following Diagram 1. Rip Slats and cut to length. Cut Spacers and Legs. Other piece will be cut after bottoms are assembled.

Materials

1/4 sheet, or scraps, 3/4" cabinet grade birch veneer plywood
1 - 2' length piano hinge
1/4" dowels
Waterproof wood glue
Polyurethane varnish

Turpentine or paint thinner
Sandpaper, fine/80 grit
Fine steel wool

Tools

Table saw or radial arm saw, for
    cutting slats
Electric circular saw with hollow
    ground plywood blade
Electric variable speed drill with ¼″
    auger-type bit
Router with ¾″ straight bit
Belt sander
Bar clamps
Awl or ice pick
Screwdriver appropriate to screws that
    come with piano hinges

Cut dowels into 2½″ lengths. Using hack saw, cut hinges to fit Top A and Top B. **NOTE:** Piano hinges come with pre-drilled holes 2 inches apart; cut hinges exactly between holes for ease of handling.

Assembly

Assemble two slatted bottoms by clamping and gluing Slats and Spacers together. When glue is dry, sand face smooth and trim edges with belt sander and table saw, to get slatted bottoms to the right size.

Measure and cut Sides and Divider to match depth of slatted bottoms. With router and ¾″ bit, cut ⅛″ deep dado grooves in Sides and on both sides of Divider.

Prop Sides and Divider up in bar clamps and slide bottoms into dado grooves. Pull bar clamps together and cut Front and Back to length of clamped assembly. **NOTE:** Back dimension is 3/16″ narrower than Front, to accommodate hinge. Glue and clamp Front and Back to Sides and Divider. When glue is dry, drill ¼″ holes approximately 2½″ deep and 2″ apart along glued joints. Apply glue to holes and dowel lengths; tap dowels into holes. When dry, sand dowel ends until smooth and flush with surface.

Glue Legs in place. Measure and cut Top pieces to fit cabinet. Using awl or ice pick to start screw holes, attach hinges to rear edges of Tops; attach Tops to cabinet.

Finishing

Using a mixture of 1 part turpentine or paint thinner to 3 parts polyurethane varnish, finish linen cabinet with three coats. Allow each coat to dry thoroughly. Lightly sand between each coat, and buff lightly with steel wool after final coat.

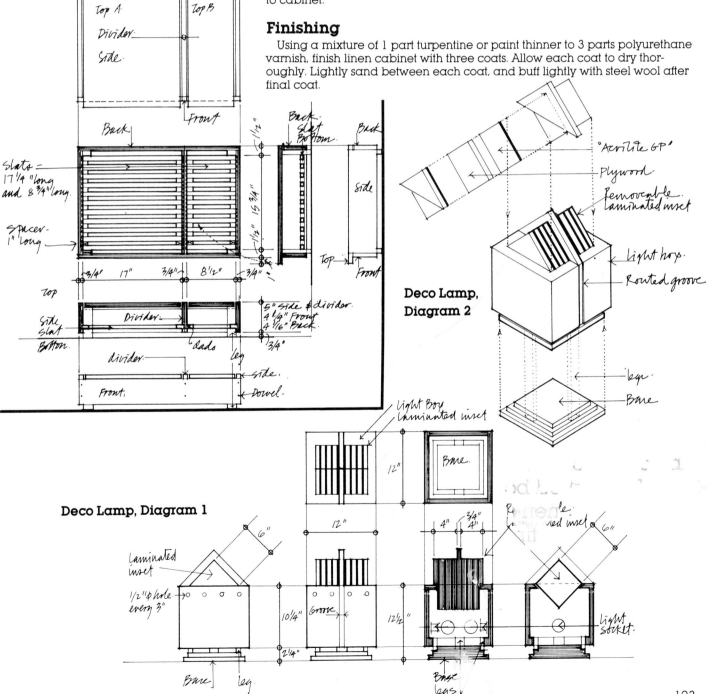

Linen Cabinet

Deco Lamp, Diagram 2

Deco Lamp, Diagram 1

Adapt Wall Fixtures to Free-Standing Lamps